SCOTLAND

Edited by Nicola Strazzullo

F

FRANCES LINCOLN LIMITED
PUBLISHERS

Acknowledgements

Introductions by Archie Miles

Site entries written by Sheila Ashton

Field researchers: Jill Aitken, Bob Black, Mike Carter, Cassie Cowie, Carol Crawford, Colin McCulloch, Duncan Kervell, Felicity Martin, Alan Melrose, Peter Norman, Andrea Partridge, Peter Quelch, Margaret Thorne, Meriel Young.

Desk researchers: Alper Akgul, Karen Bailey, Graham Livermore.

Editor: Nicola Strazzullo

Proofreader: Beatrix Mcintyre

Designer: Becky Clarke

Maps by Linda M Dawes, Belvoir Cartographics & Design

Regional maps created using Maps in Minutes data ©MAPS IN MINUTES™/ Collins Bartholomews 2007

Thanks to everyone who assisted in the production of this guide, including site owners/managers and personnel from all the organisations and privately-owned sites mentioned, particularly staff at the Woodland Trust Scotland – especially Andy Fairbairn, Angela Douglas, Jacqui Morris, Tim Hall, Roy Barlow, Jane Begg, Jill Aitken, James Gilmour, Philip Gordon, Paul Young and Adam Wallace.

Special thanks to Graham Blight and Ian White at the Woodland Trust and John Nicoll at Frances Lincoln.

We would like to thank everyone who supplied us with and gave us kind permission to use the images in this guide.

Frances Lincoln Ltd
4 Torriano Mews
Torriano Avenue
London NW5 2RZ
www.franceslincoln.com

Scotland
Copyright © Frances Lincoln 2008
Text © Woodland Trust 2008
Maps © see above

First Frances Lincoln edition: 2008

A catalogue record for this book is available from the British Library.

ISBN 978-0-7112-2669-2

Printed and bound in Singapore
The paper used in this book was sourced from sustainable forests, managed according to FSC (Forest Stewardship Council) guidelines.

1 2 3 4 5 6 7 8 9

Half title page
Ledmore and Migdale, Highlands
© Andy Fairbairn
Title page Darnaway Forest, Moray
© Jamie Cowie

Contents

MAP 1

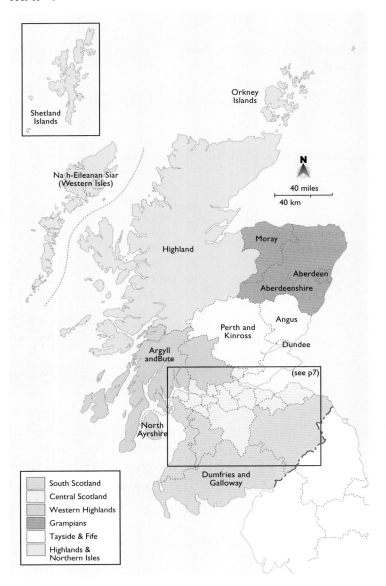

Shetland Islands

Orkney Islands

Na h-Eileanan Siar (Western Isles)

Highland

Moray

Aberdeen

Aberdeenshire

Angus

Perth and Kinross

Dundee

Argyll and Bute

(see p7)

North Ayrshire

Dumfries and Galloway

N

40 miles
40 km

	South Scotland
	Central Scotland
	Western Highlands
	Grampians
	Tayside & Fife
	Highlands & Northern Isles

MAP 2

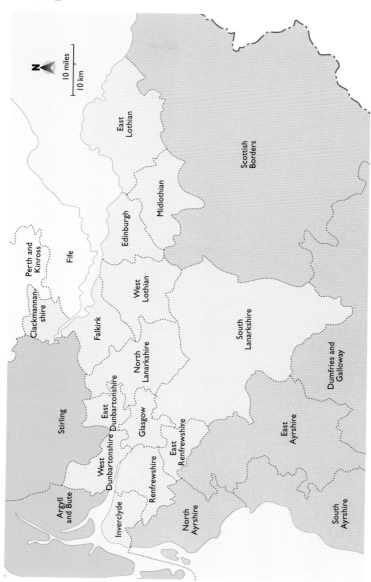

How to use this guide

Covering woods across the whole of Scotland, this book is divided into six sections, representing each of the major regions: South Scotland, Central Scotland, Western Highlands, Grampians, Tayside & Fife, the Highlands and Northern Isles.

Each section has its own introduction, a list of the featured sites, a map showing their location, and then the woodland entries themselves.

To save space and include more woods, we have grouped some sites together, either because they are close together location-wise or because the same organisation is responsible for them.

Despite this, the sheer wealth of wonderful sites means that we cannot, unfortunately, cover all the beautiful woods of Scotland in one book, so the ones featured here represent only a selection of the best. Nevertheless, if you feel a particularly great example is missing, the please feel free to recommend it. There is a form at the back of this book on page 188 which you can use to do so. We may include your suggestion when we revise this guide.

For the same reason, we haven't included site directions, but have listed the nearest town, city or village to help you find each wood.

You can get additional help finding sites by putting the relevant grid reference into an online mapping program (eg www.multimap.com at a scale of 1:25,000) and/or consulting the relevant organisation. There is a list of telephone numbers and website addresses, where available, at the back of this book on page 190. Website addresses for privately-owned sites, where available, are given next to the relevant site entry. See 'Getting there' on page 189 for more information.

Key

Type of wood

Mainly broadleaved woodland

Mainly coniferous woodland

Mixed woodland

Car parking

Parking on site

Parking nearby

Parking difficult to find

Site facilities

Sign at entry

Information board

One or more paths suitable for
  wheelchair users

Dogs not allowed*

Waymarked trail

Toilet

Picnic area

Entrance/car park charge

Refreshments on site

* Dogs are allowed at most outdoor places
in Scotland, provided under control.

Official status**

National Nature Reserve   NNR

National Park   NP

National Scenic Area   NSA

Site of Special Scientific Interest   SSSI

** Where the above designations are used,
it may indicate that either all or part of a site
is included in the designation or the site may
form part of a larger area which is designated.
The above designations are not an
exhaustive list.

Abbreviations

Forestry Commission Scotland   FSC

Hectare   HA

National Trust Scotland   NTS

Royal Society for the
  Protection of Birds   RSPB

Scottish National Heritage   SNH

Scottish Wildlife Trust   SWT

Woodland Trust Scotland   WTS

Useful tips

Scotland is a great place to go walking, with beautiful and breathtaking scenery. However, please remember that some sites can be quite remote and weather conditions can change quickly. Follow these simple tips to have a safe and enjoyable trip.

Be prepared for the worst weather and make sure you've got the right clothing and kit for the terrain. 'Four seasons in an hour' is not rare, particularly in the Highlands.

A mobile, especially with GPS, is a useful addition; but never rely solely on gadgets; phone signals can be patchy at best and GPSs won't work under heavy cloud or tree cover. Always take a map and a compass with you.

If travelling by car on remote roads take particular care. Remember to check your vehicle's fuel before you set off as, in some areas, filling stations can be a long way apart . . . as can public conveniences.

In remote areas, take plenty of water and some food with you, in case you get stranded for any length of time.

Make sure someone knows where you are going, what route you will be following and when you expect to be back.

In the summer months, make sure you have lots of midge repellent.

Some sites are fragile due to their wildlife or archaeological interest. Always follow the Scottish Outdoor Access Code (SOAC).

Visit: www.outdooraccess-scotland.com

The trees and woods of Scotland

© Andrew Barrie

Darrock Wood, Perth and Kinross

Scottish trees and woods have a long and turbulent history.

The rise and fall of Scotland's native woods is linked initially to climatic changes after the last Ice Age and later on to man's use of the land – with his desire to exploit native timber, to introduce livestock, and latterly to plant large areas of land for commercial forestry, usually with introduced species.

However, in a handful of upland refuges the native tree species, which first colonised after the ice withdrew, can still be discovered – such as remarkable dwarf colonies of birch and willows – miniature woodlands sometimes only a few feet high.

Thousands of years ago the famed Caledonian Forest covered much of the highlands – although the true extent of this forest, which was traditionally thought almost continuous from coast to coast, is now considered to have been much more fragmented and to have weathered many phases of expansion and contraction in size.

Over the last three hundred years Scotland's treescape has changed radically as timber resources became increasingly pivotal to the economy of the nation and, more specifically, the mainstay of many large estates.

With the industrial revolution came a huge demand for coppice wood – to make charcoal to fire the forges and to tan bark for a burgeoning leather industry. Oak woods became the indispensable sources for these industries, and it's due to a continual round of coppice management that many of Scotland's oak-dominated woods have survived. Some of the most fascinating and picturesque examples of these being the 'Atlantic' oak woods of the west coast, where woodlands drip with mosses, lichens and ferns in the warm, damp conditions.

During the 19th century particularly, Scottish woodland was under intense pressure, not just from the need for timber, but also from the hugely increased flocks of sheep and herds of cattle and deer. With little or no control, the livestock pinned back much of the natural regeneration of woodlands, leaving an unsustainable landscape and economy for many people. Much of the native Scottish woodland that survives to this day is there because the terrain was simply too steep and inaccessible for these animals and, to some degree, the foresters too. The deer can still be a problem in some woods, but modern management techniques and an acute awareness of conservation are now giving native woodland a much better chance.

The signature tree of Scotland is the ubiquitous Scots pine. The oldest and craggiest veteran Scots pines still grow in a handful of highland forests – mighty trees with their blue-green needles and ruddy, plated bark.

Whether pine or broadleaf, the native woodland of Scotland is most often characterised by the accompaniment of birch – a great opportunistic coloniser and an incredibly graceful tree, which so often makes a perfect visual foil for the pine, either in emerald spring attire or golden autumn glory. Birch is not usually considered a tree

© Margaret Thorne

Dawyck, Scottish Borders

of great longevity, but in Scotland it is possible to find huge old trees with a truly veteran appearance.

The two other natives that are an indelible part of the Scottish treescape are rowan and aspen, both of which make their own colourful contributions in spring and autumn.

Three of our most familiar 'naturalised' broadleaf trees also make their mark in Scotland: Sycamore appears to reach its peak of perfection in this landscape. Often reviled south of the border, in Scotland, sycamore has long been recognised as a valuable timber, shelter and shade tree, and it seems particularly suited to the northerly climate, growing to prodigious proportions. Many fine specimens grace the great houses.

Well north of its native range, beech long ago established a vibrant presence through natural regeneration in the lowlands, but its uses for timber, hedging, avenues and as a fine spreading amenity tree have caused it to be planted widely as well.

Sweet chestnut appears mainly as large specimen trees, sometimes 400–500 years old in the policy woods, but is rarely an element of coppiced woods, unlike south-east England.

The owners of Scotland's grand houses and castles have performed excellent service to the nation's trees. Scottish landowners have long held a deep affection for their trees, including a comprehensive knowledge of the many introduced conifers and their commercial potential; a reputation so well recognised that many English and Welsh landowners also employed Scottish foresters to run their estates from the 18th century onwards.

Many of Britain's most influential conifers first found favour in Scotland, due in no small measure to the remarkable endeavours of David Douglas. His most versatile introduction, the Sitka spruce, is still a mainstay of commercial forestry. The largest and earliest known plantings of Douglas fir, dating back to 1827, still thrive.

The very first Wellingtonians, the giant redwoods of California, brought over by another Scot – John Matthew, first took root in Scottish soil back in 1853.

Perhaps rivalling the Sitka in its commercial importance is the larch. Although grown in England as a decorative species from the

© Peter Norman

Wellingtonians at Drumlanrig Castle, Dumfries and Galloway

17th century, it was the millions planted by the Duke of Atholl that cemented its place both in the timber industry and the upland vistas of the landscape from the early 18th century onwards.

The contrast between ancient broadleaf woods and vast tracts of conifers may seem immense, but it's simply a matter of understanding what woodland signifies as a whole, in terms of rural economy, cultural heritage and habitat biodiversity, in order to appreciate and enjoy every aspect of the treescape.

The variety and splendour of woodland packed into this little book will give you a great sense of what's out there and, hopefully, an even greater urge to get out and explore.

ARCHIE MILES

SOUTH SCOTLAND

© East Ayrshire Council Countryside Services Section

Ness Glen

The overriding impression of South Scotland is justifiably one of rolling mountain and moor cloaked in conifers, plus one giant timber farm, but with a little perseverance there is much more to discover there.

There are some beautiful broadleaf woods, usually closely allied to the rivers, where the rush of water, lush vegetation and stunning vistas make for memorable days out. There is also a host of impressive castles and houses with beautiful gardens and parkland bedecked with trees – often species of an exotic and sometimes tender nature, thriving in the warm climate, particularly of the south-west, with its attendant Gulf Stream.

The conifer forests offer space to let your hair down, room to ride, orienteer, hurtle round dramatic mountain bike courses, or to simply take a long, refreshing walk.

ARCHIE MILES

Map
no.

See map overleaf for wood locations ▸▸

MAP 3 - SOUTH SCOTLAND

Please refer to page 17 for wood names and details of further information.

Dumfries and Galloway

Wood of Cree
Newton Stewart
(NX381708) 680 ha (1,680 acres)
SSSI
Royal Society for the Protection of Birds

Southern Scotland's largest ancient woodland, the Wood of Cree nature reserve lies in the very heart of the Cree Valley. A stunning array of plants and animals thrive here making it a delight at any time of year.

The woodland and river valley is richly populated with wildlife boasting, among the 113 different bird species, the region's biggest population of wood warblers, redstarts and pied flycatchers. More than 300 different plant species have been recorded here, plus over 31 species of mammal – including water shrews, pine martens, seven bat species and numerous otters – which can be enjoyed from a viewing platform overlooking the River Cree.

Drama is provided by the deep gorges, created by tumbling streams – and the scenic Pulhowan waterfall – which cuts through the coppiced oak and hazel-dominated wood, forming a haven for rare mosses and liverworts.

The woodland dates back to the last Ice Age and has been regularly managed by coppicing since at least 1630 until the mid 19th century. Much of it was clear felled in 1920 following the Great War. Today the trees are dense but quite spindly. However, it has benefited from recent restoration work, which has seen 40 hectares (99 acres) of conifers removed to encourage the native oaks to thrive.

Visitors can enjoy the site via two waymarked trails, both of them steep in places, so stout footwear is a must.

© Peter Norman

Wood of Cree

© Peter Norman

Glentrool Woodlands

Glentrool Woodlands
Newton Stewart
(NX415804) 78 ha (193 acres)
SSSI
Forestry Commission Scotland
and the Cree Valley Community
Woodlands Trust

The rugged beauty of the
Galloway Hills forms a
stunning backcloth for a small
group of interlinked
community oak woods lining
the banks of Loch Trool within
the Galloway Forest Park.

Access through the woods is
mainly via an often rough track
but it's worth it for the rich
wildlife and stunning setting.

Seasoned walkers can visit all
three Glentrool oakwoods –
Buchan, Glenhead and Caldons
– on a 9 km (5.5 mile) circular
walk of the loch taking in the
conifer forests to its south.
It is also possible to taken in
Buchan and Glentrool from
a shorter walk via the main
car park.

© Peter Norman

Ken-Dee Marshes

Ken-Dee Marshes
Castle Douglas
(NX699684) 79 ha (171 acres)
SSSI
Royal Society for the Protection of Birds

Quietly attractive, Ken-Dee Marshes by Loch Ken is a series of small, contrasting woodland and wetland habitats, bursting with wildlife. This can be viewed from two hides – look out for breeding redstarts, buzzards, white-fronted geese, red kites and otters.

Discover also some the region's largest oaks and a good mix of ground flora. Orchard Wood within the marshes is carpeted in bluebells, and in autumn, red squirrels often feed on trackside hazels.

23

© Peter Norman

Dalbeattie Forest

Dalbeattie Forest

Dalbeattie

(NX837600) 1,093 ha (2,700 acres)

Forestry Commission Scotland

Forming part of the Forests of the Solway Coast, with outdoor activities, scenic views, a pretty loch and wildlife around every corner – including nightjars, red squirrels and five species of bat – Dalbeattie Forest has it all. A wealth of tracks, trails and recreational facilities make this a popular destination. Visitors can walk along good footpaths dotted with features – from sculptures to an ancient hill fort.

Nearby the richly populated Mabie Forest (NX950711), a blend of conifer and broadleaves, offers similar pleasures, with a host of family activities, such as looking out for butterflies along the Lochaber Trail, which passes through Mabie Nature Reserve.

Aldouran Glen
Leswalt, nr Stranraer
(NX010635) 13 ha (32 acres)
Woodland Trust Scotland

A really lovely ancient wood, with the remains of an Iron Age hill fort at its heart, Aldouran Glen is a mix of old and mature broadleaves, dominated by sycamore and beech.

It is thought that the burn running through the glen supported otters in the past, hence the name Aldouran Glen, which means 'Glen of the Otter'. However, today you're more likely to see roe deer, than otters, while birds to try and spot include wren, long-tailed tit, coal tit, robin, treecreeper and chaffinch.

The wood is at its most colourful in May, when it is carpeted with bluebells. Other plants include greater woodrush, lady fern, ramsons, wild garlic, dog's mercury and enchanter's-nightshade. There's also a mosaic of shrubs – honeysuckle, wild raspberry and bramble – mosses, such as mouse-tail and forest star, plus liverworts and lichens, some of which are relatively uncommon.

As you walk around, look out also for dragonflies in the more open, sunny clearings.

Aldouran Glen

© WTPL/David Lund

25

Carstramon Wood
Gatehouse of Fleet

(NX592605) 72 ha (175 acres)
SSSI, NSA
Scottish Wildlife Trust

The largest, most accessible of Fleet Valley's broadleaved woods, historic Carstramon Wood is an ancient oak wood renowned for its spectacular springtime bluebell display. One of its most unusual features is the number of impressive beech trees at its centre, their origins something of a mystery.

Home to redstart, wood warbler, pied flycatcher and great spotted woodpecker, it comes alive with birdsong in spring and early summer. While the wetter parts, dominated by ash and alder, are important locally for breeding birds.

A number of marked routes, along occasionally steep and muddy woodland paths, provide access through the wood where roe deer abound and red squirrels can sometimes be spotted.

© Peter Norman

Carstramon Wood

26

Stenhouse Wood

Stenhouse Wood
Thornhill
(NX795930) 18 ha (45 acres) SSSI
Scottish Wildlife Trust

Stenhouse Wood is set on the slopes of picturesque Shinnel Glen. This little-visited peaceful wood is a delightful site, renowned for its wildlife. Dominated by ash, elm and oak, it boasts a couple of local specialities; toothwort – a parasitic spring-flowering plant that lives off elm and hazel; and bird's nest orchid – which can be found beneath the beech in June – for those lucky enough to spot it. Red squirrels are occasionally found here and birdlife also abounds on site. The wood supports pied flycatchers and wood warblers, while Shinnel Water, which flows past the wood, is frequented by dippers and grey wagtails.

It's well worth combining a tour of Stenhouse with visits to the ancient hill top fort of Tynron Doon, just across the glen, Tynron Juniper Wood (NX827928), and the nearby Drumlanrig Castle and Country Park (see below).

27

© Peter Norman

Drumlanrig Castle and Country Park

Drumlanrig Castle and Country Park
Thornhill

(NX851993) 50,000 ha (123,600 acres)

Privately owned

www.drumlanrig.co.uk

Home to one of Scotland's largest sycamores and the first Douglas fir ever planted in Great Britain, 17th-century treasure trove Drumlanrig Castle, part of the Buccleuch Estates, is an imposing sandstone mansion by the River Nith, set in historic woods and parkland.

The estate is dotted with small lochs, ponds and burns with many parkland trees dating back to the 18th century. There's an abundance of wildlife, including red squirrels, otters and barn owls. Public needs are also well catered for with gardens, cycle routes and recreational facilities.

Lochwood
Moffat
(NY085972) 10 ha (27 acres) SSSI
**Privately owned by the Annandale
Estate**

It might be a small oak wood,
but Lockwood is packed with
treasures because virtually
every tree is an ancient, gnarled
and twisted veteran, drenched
in ferns, mosses and rare
lichens. There are no paths but
most of the notable trees can
be enjoyed from a minor road
running through the wood,
offering glimpses of
woodpeckers, nuthatches and
pied flycatchers, along with roe
and fallow deer. Look out also
for the 12th-century motte
earthworks and nearby, the
remains of a 15th-century
castle.

Lochwood
© Peter Norman

29

© Peter Norman

Gallow Hill

Gallow Hill
Moffat
(NT086065) 60 ha (148 acres)
Privately owned

Gallow Hill is a mixed plantation perched on a hill overlooking the popular tourist town of Moffat. Its name adds weight to the long-held belief that this was once a site of executions. Today life is quieter and the wood is surrounded by pastures and smaller woods.

Much of the site is classified as ancient woodland and has retained its characteristic ground flora, despite some exotic broadleaves and conifers and the dominance of rhododendron in the under-storey, which is now being controlled. In May the wood is carpeted with bluebells and ferns, greater woodrush and ramsons, and other, more uncommon, species.

From the broadleaved perimeter of the wood, accessed via a circular footpath, you can enjoy excellent views of the surrounding countryside.

Galloway House Gardens
Garlieston
(NX478452) 20 ha (60 acres)
Privately owned
www.gallowayhousegardens.co.uk

A scenic highlight in a grassed landscape, Galloway House Gardens is an informal woodland garden, dominated by rhododendron but boasting a number of rare species.

Well-maintained paths give good access to all areas including a pleasant walk to the seashore, past ancient oaks, beech trees, a restored ornamental pond and the ruins of Gruggleton Castle.

Galloway House Gardens
© Peter Norman

Wamphray Glen
Moffat
(NY121961) 8 ha (20 acres)
The Crown Estates

The densely wooded Wamphray Glen, is a small, attractive narrow glen that boasts a circular walk of about 5 km (3 miles) with bridges, kissing gates and a series of low waterfalls from Wamphray Water, which runs through it. It's rich in local history and adjacent is the site of a fortified Anglo-Norman motte and bailey castle.

The privately-owned South Turnmuir Plantation (NY121809) also resides not far away, on the edge of Lockerbie town centre. This pine-dominated wood is home to roe deer, foxes and red squirrels and, although most of the trees were planted in the last 50 years, a number of individual coniferous and deciduous trees date back more than 100 years. It offers easy woodland walks and access to the Lockerbie Wildlife Trusts' Eskrigg Reserve, which lies within.

Wamphray Glen
© Peter Norman

Scottish Borders

Glentress
Peebles
(NT284397) 1,137 ha (2,800 acres)
SSSI (Tweed catchment)
Forestry Commission Scotland

Historic Glentress, a mammoth forest and conifer plantation famed for its mountain bike trails and ospreys, is the top visitor attraction in the Scottish Borders.

Though still a commercial forest, it's a major draw for family visitors who make full use of its easy, well-cared for paths, eight waymarked walking trails, mountain-bike rides and excellent facilities, including a bike hire shop and café.

Other attractions include a stand of 100-year old Douglas firs, wildlife ponds, a good variety of autumn fungi and a host of typical woodland birds, including buzzard, wood pigeon, goldcrest, chaffinch, crossbill and, in more open areas, kestrels and owls. Squirrels and roe deer have also made Glentress their home.

History is never far away with the remains of several Iron Age hill forts and a reconstructed Iron Age roundhouse. The nearby Tweeddale museum and gallery is also worth visiting, as is the St Ronan's Well interpretation centre at Innerleithen.

Glentress
© Margaret Thorne

Dawyck Botanic Garden
Peebles

(NT167352) 24 ha (60 acres) NSA
Royal Botanic Garden, Edinburgh
www.rbge.org.uk

One of the finest arboretums in the world, thanks to more than 300 years of tree planting, Dawyck Botanic Garden is an excellent place to learn about trees and woodland.

Set in a picturesque glen on the northern edge of the Tweedsmuir Hills, with fine valley views and delightful burnside walks, the magical year-round setting features an outstanding collection of native and exotic trees, while offering a first-hand insight of a wealth of woodland plants, including mosses, lichens, ferns and fungi.

Please note that no dogs, except guide dogs, are allowed.

Dawyck
Botanic
Garden
© Margaret
Thorne

33

Plora Wood
© WTPL/Pat herbert

Plora Wood
Innerleithen
(NT345366) 21 ha (52 acres) SSSI
Woodland Trust Scotland

With a peaceful and intimate feel, the ancient wooded slopes of Plora Wood, above the rich alluvial floodplain of the River Tweed, provide glimpses across the Tweed Valley beyond.

An accessible and attractive broadleaf wood, Plora features a mix of oak, beech, ash and sycamore and is one of the five largest oak woods in the Scottish Borders. In fact, it represents more than half the ancient oak wood in Tweedale.

In spring and summer, wild flowers abound here, including primrose, bluebells, wood anemone, figwort and the unusual upland enchanter's nightshade with its toothed leaves. Delicate yellow tormentil also grows beneath the gnarled and twisted oaks, its woody roots once used to cure stomach ache. The birdlife is equally varied, ranging from chiffchaff and redstart, to goldcrest and green woodpecker.

Nearby, you'll also find another Woodland Trust Scotland site. St Ronan's Wood (NT328372), which includes part of Caerlee Hill Fort and is well worth a visit while in the area.

Newcastleton Forest
Hawick
(NY506881) 3,000 ha (7,413 acres)
Forestry Commission Scotland

Stunning scenery, a magical blend of adventure and tranquillity, a wealth of wildlife and excellent facilities… it's all here at Priesthill, the beautiful heart of Newcastleton Forest in the Liddel Valley.

A great family day out, the site features mature woods of spruce and larch, alongside grassy slopes, wetlands, ponds

© Margaret Thorne

Newcastleton Forest

and a smattering of broadleaf trees. The area is rich in archaeology, from Iron Age forts and mediaeval settlements to a 5000-year-old Long Cairn, where the ancients buried their dead in stone-lined chambers.

Mountain bikers can take their pick of four brilliant bike routes while walkers can stroll along gently sloping paths beside the Priesthill Burn and around the ponds, where dragonflies provide welcome summer entertainment. A hide overlooking Liddel Valley offers the opportunity to observe badgers at close hand, and there's even the chance to watch buzzards soaring or listen to the calls of moorland birds as you pass by.

There is also much to explore in the nearby Craik Forest (NT353080). At 4,000 hectares (9,900 acres), this large maturing conifer plantation is stunning to look at and bursting with wildlife.

Pine, larch and Norway spruce, favoured by the red squirrel, grow around the many burns that flow through the site, while some of forest trees are almost 100 years old. Take your pick of trails – check out stunning panoramic views or discover waterfalls nestling in hidden glens.

35

Pease Dean

Dunbar

(NT790704) 33 ha (82 acres) SSSI

Scottish Wildlife Trust

Pease Dean is a precious fragment of ancient sessile oak woodland, the largest of its kind in Berwickshire. A rich mix of native broadleaves, plus planted conifers and towering sycamores, create dense canopies in some sections of the wood. It features an interesting mix of plants and animals, including ancient woodland flora with national rarities, including mosses and liverworts. Two burns flow through the site and twin wooded valleys open out to a broad grassy area, set against the attractive backdrop of sea and a sandy bay.

© Margaret Thorne

Pease Dean

© Margaret Thorne

Bowhill House and Country Park

Bowhill House and Country Park

Bowhill

(NT428278)

27,000 ha (67,000 acres)

Privately owned

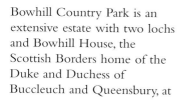

Bowhill Country Park is an extensive estate with two lochs and Bowhill House, the Scottish Borders home of the Duke and Duchess of Buccleuch and Queensbury, at its heart. The mix of policy woodland and commercial plantation, from which there are some grand views of the house and the estate, is rich in wildlife, flora and fauna.

There are good family facilities, four tranquil woodland walks and interesting features include three fine beeches, dating back more than 200 years and some of Scotland's oldest Douglas firs and giant Redwoods.

37

South Ayrshire

Ayr Gorge Woodland
Mauchline
(NS457249) 46 ha (114 acres) SSSI
Scottish Wildlife Trust

Dominated by oak and birch, but dotted with ash, elm and conifers, Ayr Gorge ranks among one of Ayrshire's most important woodland habitats, being one of the finest native woods in the region. A romantic haven where man and wildlife are equally at home, it's a place of drama and romance – said to be the site where Burns met Highland Mary to make their ill-fated arrangements for their departure from Scotland together, halted, unfortunately, by her death.

Lush woodland envelopes a steep, picturesque sandstone gorge where kingfishers, spotted flycatchers, dippers and great spotted woodpeckers make their home. Otters, badgers, bats and roe deer thrive here, along with an impressive array of flora and fungi. The presence of common cow-wheat, woodrush and wood fescue, along with longhorn beetles bear testament to the site's ancient woodland status.

There's little wonder it's such a popular draw for families as the site has a good network of well-maintained paths – now part of the River Ayr Way. Choose from a range of short or longer scenic woodland walks and be rewarded with attractive views of the reserve.

Ayr Gorge Woodland
© Carol Crawford

Blairquhan
Maybole
(NS379049) 400 ha (1,000 acres)
Privately owned
www.blairquhan.co.uk

A small, traditional Scottish estate, Blairquhan lies in the picturesque Girvan Valley, at the northern end of the Galloway Forest Park. A collection of rare trees, including one of Scotland's finest heritage trees, the Dool Tree of Blairquhan, which was used for hangings in feudal times, can be found on site. You may also see red squirrels, otters, kingfishers, buzzards and ravens – all frequent visitors. A tree trail is provided through the estate's pinetum and walled garden, access to which is available every Sunday from Easter to September or by prior appointment.

Culzean Castle and Country Park
Maybole
(NS233103) 227 ha (563 acres) SSSI
National Trust for Scotland

Record numbers of people visit the history-steeped coastal woodlands and other visitor attractions, including the spectacular cliff-top Culzean Castle, of Scotland's first Country Park. With some of the best coastal deciduous woodland in southern Scotland, its miles of woodland walks linking both land and sea, afford wonderful views. The coastal belt, dominated by wind-shaped, cliff-top ash and sycamores, shelters an inland mosaic of mixed-age natural woodland and designed woodland garden, providing a diverse range of habitats for wildlife.

Culzean Castle and Country Park
© Carol Crawford

East Ayrshire

Ness Glen
Dalmellington
(NS476014) 18 ha (45 acres) SSSI
Privately owned

Described as 'one of the Britain's finest examples of a true rock gorge', attractive Ness Glen, part of the Craigengillan Estate, has year-round appeal thanks to high humidity levels, which keep it green and pleasant in all seasons. Mosses, liverworts, lichens and ferns thrive throughout the year and the site also supports deer, red squirrels, woodland birds and a variety of flowers. On the lower slopes the woodland is mainly ash and elm, with oak and birch on the upper slopes.

A fast-flowing river, with rapids and falls, lends extra excitement to the glen, with trees clinging to near vertical rocks that are dotted along the route of the river. Then, closer to the open moorland and Loch Doon there are some impressive views.

Recent work has created a 3.2 km (2 mile) circuit walk around Loch Doon, though you need to take care along the lower path which is damp and vulnerable to landslips.

Ness Glen

© East Ayrshire Council Countryside Services Section

Woodroad Park
Cumnock

(NS570206) 19 ha (47 acres)

East Ayrshire Council

www.eastayrshirewoodlands.co.uk

Woodroad Park straddles Lugar Water and includes ancient and semi-natural woodland, as well as a substantial area of amenity grassland known as 'the holm'.

It provides excellent mature habitats for a range of species, including tawny owls, great spotted woodpeckers, jays, song thrushes and treecreepers, while migrant visitors include willow warblers, blackcaps and chiffchaffs.

During spring and summer, the woodland floor is resplendent with the contrasting colours of species like wood anemone, wood sorrel, bluebell and red campion, while the mature woodland provides excellent roosting and feeding habitat for bats.

The woodland incorporates a network of footpaths developed by East Ayrshire Woodlands, as part of the Millennium Forest for Scotland project. A new path has recently been developed through Broombraes to the north, which is accessed from beneath the dramatic viaduct. Please take care as some paths are steep in places, with steps that could pose problems for less-able visitors.

Woodroad Park

© Carol Crawford

© Carol Crawford

Dean Castle Country Park

Dean Castle Country Park
Kilmarnock
(NS437394) 80 ha (200 acres)
East Ayrshire Council
www.deancastle.com

Dubbed Kilmarnock's 'secret gem', Dean Castle Country Park has woodland walks to suit all ages and abilities. The estate features open parkland, woodland plantations, historic buildings and riverside walks.

Fox, roe deer, woodland songbirds and a good range of flora abound, including spring bluebells. There are some large old specimen trees to enjoy within the grounds and the park's more recent attractions are a Discovery Centre and an auditorium. The castle itself is steeped in history and noted for its weaponry and armour collections.

North Ayrshire

Kelburn Castle and Country Centre

Largs

(NS217567) 300 ha (741 acres)

Privately owned

www.kelburncountrycentre.com

A delight for the young, and young at heart, 13th-century Kelburn Castle, home of the Earls of Glasgow, lies at the heart of an estate that marries history, nature, adventure and romance, into a great family day out.

The estate has many natural and historical features, including two of Scotland's 100 heritage trees. The glen, said to be one of Scotland's most beautiful natural woods, has a mixture of native trees, exotic planting, burns, waterfalls, deep gorges and spectacular vistas.

Kelburn Castle and Country Centre

© Carol Crawford

43

Corsehillmuir Wood
Kilwinning
(NS315435) 27 ha (67 acres)
Scottish Wildlife Trust

Nature lovers will appreciate the wild, yet quiet, character of this mixed broadleaved woodland next to the extensive Eglinton Country Park. Rich in wildlife, a variety of woodland birds and 150 different plant species have been recorded on site.

A range of trees can be found here, including an ancient crab apple and many other dry and wet woodland species. Though most trees are just 50 years old, coppiced oaks and regenerating birch of all ages bear testament to a longer history of woodland cover.

Corsehillmuir Wood

© Carol Crawford

The Isle of Arran

Glenashadale
Whiting Bay
(NS030250) 40 ha (99 acres)
Forestry Commission Scotland

Surrounded by a large commercial forestry plantation, stunning Glenashdale is a forest rich in natural and archaeological heritage and hailed as one of the Forestry Commission's top ten British forest walks. Highlights include the Glenashdale Waterfall and 'The Giants' Graves', a group of Neolithic chambered cairns. Visitors can enjoy its two spectacular waterfalls, at their best in rain and accessed via a well-maintained, occasionally steep path. There are two entrances from Whiting Bay, one at the Coffee Pot and the other at Ashdale bridge.

Goatfell and Brodick Country Park
Isle of Arran
(NS010380) 72 ha (177 acres) & 2,283 ha (5,639 acres) SSSI, NSA
National Trust Scotland

Encompassing Arran's major peaks, Goatfell is a walker's paradise with the granite peaks offering a whole range of walks from tourist routes to major climbs. The glacial peaks and valleys are home to red deer, golden eagles and peregrine falcons, with a wealth of geological and archaeological interest. Remnants of upland woods have been protected from grazing over the last ten years.

Meanwhile, Brodick Country Park is a mixture of grassland with mature woodland. Merkland Wood hosts the island's only remaining semi-natural woodland and is home to red squirrels, great spotted woodpeckers, badgers and otters. A trail map guides the visitor through the 11 km (6.8 miles) of walks, which give great views of spectacular gorges and waterfalls.

CENTRAL SCOTLAND

© Clyde Muirshiel Regional Park

Clyde Muirshiel Regional Park

A glance at the map shows this area, largely dominated by the conurbations of Glasgow and Edinburgh, to be not particularly well endowed with green bits, yet there are a host of beautiful woods and parks to be found.

Not quite as expansive as those in the Scottish Borders, these sites still pack plenty of interest. Some of the broadleaf woodlands have managed to retain vestiges of their working heritage – ancient pollards and coppice stools, a legacy of fine old trees, often several hundred years old, but long since neglected since the industries they once supported have disappeared.

Country Parks are a big feature of this region and they admirably combine the many recreational requirements for a wide cross-section of visitors. Whether it's whizzing around on a bike or strolling quietly with toddlers and buggies, there's somewhere just right for you.

ARCHIE MILES

See map overleaf for wood locations ▸▸

MAP 4 - CENTRAL SCOTLAND

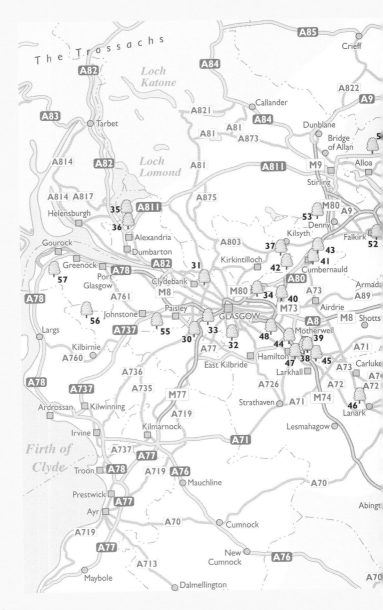

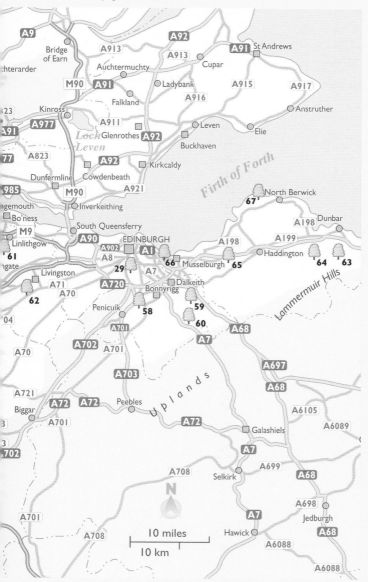

The above map is a guide only. Please contact relevant organisations for more detailed location information.

49

Edinburgh

Hermitage of Braid
Edinburgh
(NT255704) 53 ha (130 acres)
City of Edinburgh Council

Sitting right on Edinburgh's doorstep, the Hermitage of Braid is a historic turreted house, with a dramatic slice of nature, including a steep-sided river valley and habitats of woodland, grassland, scrub, freshwater and marshland.

Rich in plants and wildlife, this is a great place for many reasons – ecology, birdlife, recreation and relaxation. It's a great workout for those who enjoy walking on hilly ground, with a wealth of walks and good footpath links to Blackford Hill, which has panoramic city views.

The Braid burn runs through the centre of the site and families can enjoy picnics by babbling brooks or wander through the woodland of broadleaves and conifers (carpeted by bluebells in springtime), listen to the sounds of the rich bird population or admire the ancient trees.

The nearby woodland of Craigmillar Castle Park (NT286710) – also managed by the City of Edinburgh Council – is another rich and varied place. A complex of woods and open fields, this 65-hectare (160-acre) 'urban sanctuary' contains mixed woodland, tree avenues and young native trees. It's home to an abundance of wildlife, and is significant in both landscape and historic terms. Mary Queen of Scots once stayed at Craigmillar Castle, and admired the views across the Forth to Fife, which can still be enjoyed today.

Also managed by the City of Edinburgh Council, is Corstorphine Hill (NT205743), a 76-hectare (188-acre) woodland-covered ridge, with magnificent panoramic views.

Craigmillar Castle Park
© Meriel Young

Glasgow

Darnley Mill and Walkmill Glen
Glasgow
(NS526590) 10 ha (25 acres) SSSI
Glasgow City Council

Darnley Mill is a mosaic of woodland scrub, grassland and wetland habitats, supporting a host of animal and plant species and providing an attractive setting for walks with open views of the countryside. The nearby Walkmill Glen (NS523583) is a semi-natural woodland in a narrow valley. The steep valley sides, covered in beech, ash, sycamore, birch, hazel and rowan, can be explored via a good network of paths.

Dawsholm Park
Glasgow
(NS553695) 33 ha (82 acres)
Glasgow City Council

A lovely, large woodland park with an impressive mix of trees, some dating back hundreds of years, Dawsholm Park lies in the west end of Glasgow, where it's a big favourite with families.

This Victorian site is criss-crossed by a myriad of paths, including the Kelvinside Walkway, and is a great place to escape the city noise and enjoy the wealth of tree species, birds and excellent views of the River Kelvin. It's also great spot for outdoor sports, such as cycling, orienteering and jogging.

© Duncan Kervell

Cathkin Braes

Cathkin Braes
Glasgow
(NS608582) 199 ha (492 acres)
Glasgow City Council

With its diversity of habitats, the hillside country park of Cathkin Braes is renowned for its special views across Glasgow. Large expanses of grassland are complemented by marsh, heath, scrub and hedgerows; while the woods include some mature woodland areas, with lovely oak stands, and younger sections planted on the lower slopes. Plants and wildlife are plentiful.

Pollok Country Park
Glasgow
(NS560614) 146 ha (361 acres)
Glasgow City Council

The only country park within Glasgow, Pollok Country Park is an exceptionally attractive site, housing historic Pollok House and its associated gardens, plus extensive mature woodlands.

The woodland garden, which is served by a labyrinth of paths, also features the famous heritage tree 'The Pollok Beech'.

Over in the heart of the city's East End is the smaller, Tollcross Park (NS636638). At 37 hectares (91 acres), this scenic glen and woodland has mature native broadleaves and a host of visitor attractions, including a children's farm and international rose garden.

Bishop's Estate
Easterhouse and Garthamlock
(NS660671) 60 ha (148 acres)
SSSI (Bishop's Loch)
**Glasgow City Council and
Forestry Commission Scotland**

Bishop's Estate has six main woodlands – West Maryston, Lochend Burn, Lochwood Plantation, Craigend, Todd's Well and Cardownan – all a mix of recently established broadleaves and mature woods, some of which interlink to provide a great community resource.

The younger sites complement the rich mix of habitats around Easterhouse and Garthamlock and, between them, the sites have a wealth of visitor experiences, from views and walks to wildflower meadows, and a rich wildlife population, including roe deer, meadow pipit, water voles and northern marsh orchid.

Bishop's Estate

© Duncan Kervell

53

West Dunbartonshire

Whinny Hill
Balloch
(NS397848) 100 ha (248 acres)
NSA, NP
Woodland Trust Scotland

Whinny Hill sits atop two hills – Whinny Hill and the neighbouring Knockour Hill. A wonderfully varied wood with many acres of young broadleaves, as well as more mature mixed woodland and open space, at its highest point it rewards walkers with stunning views over Loch Lomond.

Among the 36 species of bird recorded here are skylark, song thrush, linnet, reed bunting, swallow, and the occasional visiting capercaillie. In fact, these are thought to be among the last of the true Scottish capercaillie living on the islands and the shores of Loch Lomond.

There is a wide network of tracks to explore the area and the main access point for Whinny Hill is provided through the nearby Balloch Castle Country Park (see below) a Victorian creation of woodland, parkland and ornamental gardens sloping down to the shores of Loch Lomond.

Whinny Hill
© WTPL

Balloch Castle Country Park
Balloch
(NS398827) 84 ha (200 acres) NP
West Dunbartonshire Council

A beautiful loch-side setting, gardens, woodland walks and tremendous views over Loch Lomond, make this varied country park well worth a visit. The woodland varies from natural to exotic, with large areas of natural oak and even a fairy glen. There are lots of walks, with Balloch Castle adding an impressive backdrop.

East Dunbartonshire

Twechar Wood
Kilsyth
(NS710760) 205 ha (506 acres)
Forestry Commission Scotland

A small hilltop wood nestling between two villages, Twechar Wood is steeped in history and has some fantastic Roman archaeology, including a bath house and parts of the Antonine wall.

Visitors are actively encouraged into the woodland, a mix of conifer plantation and broadleaves, which commands fine views of the local area. It can be accessed via two paths, which would benefit from some upgrading.

Twechar Wood
© Duncan Kervell

North Lanarkshire

Baron's Haugh
Wishaw
(NS755548) 104 ha (257 acres)
Royal Society for the Protection of Birds

This expansive reserve is a vast, richly populated area which guarantees bird spectacles all year round and attracts more than 25,000 visitors annually.

Nationally important for its numbers of wintering whooper swans and breeding gadwalls, it offers wonderful opportunities to observe wildlife – some 22 different mammals have been recorded here, including otters and badgers.

Woodland is an integral part of the reserve. To the east are old policy woods of mature oak, sycamore, beech, ash, lime and yew, dotted with ash and Norway maple.

The old mine works on the site bear testament to site's history – it was once part of the extensive Dalzell Estate.

© Duncan Kervell

Dalzell Estate Woodlands

Dalzell Estate Woodlands
Coatbridge

(NS761554) 40 ha (99 acres)
North Lanarkshire Council

Most of these beautiful old policy woodlands, part of the historic Dalzell Estate, are designated as important conservation areas, being either ancient semi-natural woodland or long established woodland of plantation origin.

Dalzell House forms the focal point for the estate which includes parkland, grass fields, ornamental Japanese gardens, an arboretum and the Whinney Burn valley.

Ideal for walking, cycling and riding, there are three waymarked tracks across these extensive grounds. Look out for Covenanters Oak, where a 17th-century cleric is said to have preached to 400 Covenanters.

Drumpellier Country Park
Coatbridge

(NS704664) 336 ha (830 acres)
SSSI

North Lanarkshire Council

A tranquil country park, boasting two lochs, a good range of recreational facilities and a mix of mature and young woodland, Drumpellier Country Park attracts thousands of visitors each year.

One of the lochs, Woodend, has been designated a Site of Special Scientific Interest and the waterfowl and migratory birds that use it form a major attraction; while the shores of Lochend Loch provide pleasant open views.

The woods, which have an abundance of wildflowers and a wealth of fungi, are home to many birds and other small animals. All can be discovered from a good network of paths, many suited to wheelchairs and prams.

Hints of the park's historic links are evident – yet the facilities provided here are bang up to date with water activities, a visitor centre, formal garden and children's play area.

Palacerigg Country Park
Cumbernauld
(NS772742) 80 ha (197 acres)
North Lancashire Council

Rich in wildlife, with a good choice of nature trails, Palacerigg has abundant attractions, including animal collections, nature trails, a visitor centre and tree-top walkway. The majority of the woodland at Palacerigg is conifer plantation, but to the north, the oak woods of Glencryan and its associated gorge are worth including on a longer walk through the site. The nearby 42-hectare (104-acre) Scottish Wildlife Trust site – Luggiebank Wood (NS758730) – is also worth a visit. Long, narrow and tranquil, it follows the course of Luggie Water, with small waterfalls and pools, and features some locally rare birds.

Broadwood
Cumbernauld
(NS721732) 20 ha (50 acres)
North Lanarkshire Council

Ideal for spotting wildlife, especially waterside birds, the plantation woodlands around Broadwood loch are a great place to visit, whatever your age.

These are young woodlands, well served with two walks and home to great spotted woodpecker, wren, willow warbler, long-tailed tit, roe deer and fox.

The loch is the focal point of the site, with its herons, reed bunting, pochard, swans, Canada geese and tufted ducks.

Cumbernauld Glen
Cumbernauld
(NS777763) 115 ha (284 acres)
Scottish Wildlife Trust

Steeped in history, ideal for relaxation and well-loved by local people, this lovely semi-natural woodland is part of a landscape of parkland, glens, streams and burns.

Well served by many pathways, the site was once used as a royal hunting ground and the remains of Red Comyn's 13th-century castle can still be seen by the parkland.

Today it is full of wildlife, including badgers, bats, roe deer and foxes, which thrive in the glen. Green woodpeckers, siskins, jays, blackcaps and wood warblers can also be found in abundance and the site is rich in native flora and fauna.

The ancient woodlands in the glen have great wildlife importance and are covered with vast carpets of bluebells and wild hyacinths in spring and early summer. Oak and sycamore are the dominant tree species, while many small mammals live in the undergrowth.

Cumbernauld Glen
© Duncan Kervell

Strathclyde Country Park
Motherwell
(NS727574) 337 ha (833 acres)
North Lanarkshire Council

One of Scotland's leading centres for outdoor recreation, Strathclyde Country Park lies within the River Clyde Valley.

Strathclyde loch forms the focal point for many of the park's activities, which cover everything from sailing and water skiing to birdwatching and cycling.

Strathclyde Country Park
© Duncan Kervell

The expanse of countryside also takes in wildlife refuges, open parkland, rough wetland and mature woodland, all waiting to be explored via miles of surfaced footpaths.

The woodland is found in narrow belts around the loch, and there are larger areas to the east, which is a quieter part of the park and features semi-mature and mature woodland with ample paths leading uphill to Motherwell.

Great for family days out, dog walking, camping and playing, the woods form just one part of the park experience.

Cambusnethan
Wishaw
(NS779538) 10 ha (25 acres)
North Lanarkshire Council

Cambusnethan is a mixture of young and old woodland, set around the old ruins of Cambusnethan House. The woodland lies on the Clyde escarpment and forms an intimate broadleaved setting surrounded by farmland.

The woods provide links to longer distance walks and provide good access to the escarpment overlooking the Clyde valley. Spring visitors can enjoy carpets of bluebells in the older parts of the site.

Additional woods of interest nearby include the woodlands of Colzium Estate (NS728787) also managed by North Lanarkshire Council and Wester Moffatt (NS784656), managed by the Central Scotland Forest Trust.

Much loved by local people, Colzium has a long heritage of woodlands, amenity areas, play parks, a well-developed path network, and historical buildings, which include a theatre, walled garden, castle ruins and an ice house.

A small and relatively new woodland, it has a good footpath which passes through the site down to the riverside and continues along the North Calder Heritage Trail.

South Lanarkshire

Clyde Valley Woodlands
Lanark
(NS868445) 130 ha (321 acres)
SSSI, NNR
Scottish Natural Heritage and the Scottish Wildlife Trust, plus various private owners

Stunning and rich in wildlife, the Clyde Valley Woodlands which include Lower Nethan Gorge, Garrion Gill, Cleghorn Glen and Cartland Craigs, rank among the richest broadleaved woods in Scotland.

The woods are teeming with woodland plants and birds and many of the old oaks have been moulded by nature into fantastic shapes. There are spectacularly colourful carpets of bluebells and primroses in spring and summer and it's particularly fascinating in autumn, when the diverse range of trees creates a palette of beautiful hues, while fungi and invertebrates thrive among the deadwood.

The nearby Falls of Clyde (NS882423) is another species-rich wooded gorge with spectacular waterfalls, a good network of paths and family facilities. While there, it is worth looking around the visitor centre and the historic village of New Lanark, which sits just below the falls.

There are entry signs at most sites and a network of paths, but these ancient woods do lie in deep sandstone gorges – very steep in places – so care is advised with children or dogs.

Falls of Clyde
© Carol Crawford

Chatelherault Country Park

Hamilton

(NS738540) 250 ha (617 acres)
SSSI

South Lanarkshire Council

The combination of a beautiful wooded gorge and neighbouring parkland has created a five-star tourist attraction at Chatelherault Country Park.

A wildlife haven, it's rich in ferns and mosses, and alive with colourful bluebells and wild garlic in spring, when songbirds are also plentiful. Dippers and grey wagtail, badgers, otters and bats are also at home here. There are 16 km (10 miles) of walks through ancient woodland and younger conifers, with wonderful views of the river, woods and parkland.

Chatelherault also incorporates Hamilton High Parks, which has a number of ancient oak trees, known as the Cadzow Oaks.

Chatelherault Country Park
© Carol Crawford

Bothwell Castle Grounds
© Carol Crawford

Bothwell Castle Grounds
Uddingston
(NS688594) 73 ha (180 acres) SSSI
South Lanarkshire Council

Nestling by Scotland's largest and finest 13th-century castle, this well-loved ancient woodland along the banks of the Clyde is a great place for family walks.

Riverside paths, great views, the rich sound of birdsong and easy (if occasionally muddy) walking conditions make this a huge favourite with locals.

The woods themselves are mainly native oak-birch and ash-elm combinations, with alder and willow growing by the river. Teeming with wildlife, the flora is typical of ancient woodland, with primrose and garlic thriving – but more than 330 other types of plant have been recorded here, including uncommon ones such as hellebore. In spring, the woods are a blaze of colour, with carpets of bluebells.

Heathland Forest & 'The Glen'
Forth
(NS950548) 1,000 ha (2,471 acres)
Forestry Commission Scotland

Quietly set on the outskirts of a former mining town, Heathland Forest and its smaller more peaceful neighbour, 'The Glen', is an extensive and popular forest plantation, served by an excellent network of waymarked paths. The site, once an industrial centre, is being reclaimed by woodland and wildlife following a mass of conifer planting in the 1960s. On a clear day you can see across to the Scottish Borders.

Clackmannanshire

Dollar Glen
Dollar
(NS964983) 24 ha (60 acres) SSSI
National Trust for Scotland

Dollar Glen
© Duncan Kervell

Impressive Dollar Glen is an exceptionally beautiful ancient broadleaved woodland lining a dramatic, steep ravine at the foot of the Ochil Hills.

Just a short walk from the centre of the historic town of Dollar, the site is crossed by two rivers that flow through the gorge and down the steep glen to form stunning waterfalls in the woodland heart. The formidable Castle Campbell stands proudly at the head of the glen, surrounded by woodland, giving this enchanted setting a storybook feel.

The woodland has an untouched atmosphere, due partly to the steepness of the ravines and the impressive size of the trees. Stands of mature ash, oak and sycamore, an understorey of hazel and woodrush and stunning displays of spring bluebells are all here in this mystical scene, with the sound of rivers and waterfalls ever-present. Green woodpeckers, roe deer, bluebells, ramsons and wood rush feature among the wide array of species that inhabit this site.

Walkways, an impressive series of footbridges and a pathway run through the glen, providing ample opportunities to drink in this array of stunning spectacles. The wooded glen is a great place to head for family strolls, though the walks are slightly strenuous and the steepness of the slope means exploration is challenging. However, the pathways are well maintained and reassuring.

The main path through the glen, and the most popular route to the castle, takes in the waterfalls and river views.

65

Wood Hill Wood
Alva
(NS898976) 79 ha (196 acres)
Woodland Trust Scotland

Wood Hill Wood
© WTPL/Roger Warhurst

True to its name, Wood Hill Wood rises above the village of Alva. One of the oldest plantations in Scotland, it stands out as the most extensive piece of woodland on the rocky scarp slopes of the Ochil Hills.

It was probably planted in 18th century by Sir John Erskine, a distant descendant of Robert Bruce. Today, it consists of mainly broadleaved woodland, with a blend of sycamore and ash.

It was once the site of one of Europe's richest silver ore discoveries and legend has it that 40 tonnes of silver ore are still buried somewhere nearby – their exact whereabouts long forgotten. In fact, silver can still be panned from the fast-flowing Silver Burn, which carves its way down the glen. Aspiring modern-day miners are allowed to try their hand at panning for silver at specially held events, as part of the Scottish Geological Festival.

Visitors are advised to stick to the footpaths, since the site lies on very steep slopes, but walkers on the upper part of the circular route will be rewarded by spectacular views across the forth, and may spot one of four known ancient trees, including one interesting old beech pollard. Buzzards are known to nest in the area, and in summer the wood has a carpet of dog's mercury, a plant typical of long-established woods.

Wood Hill Wood adjoins a much smaller site – the Ochil Hills Woodland Park (NS898975). Like Wood Hill, these woods, which are now managed by Clackmannanshire Council, were formerly within the grounds of Alva House, and are a good place to start before exploring further into the Ochil Hills.

Falkirk

Callendar Wood
Falkirk
(NS905792) 94 ha (232 acres)
Forestry Commission Scotland

Callendar Wood has something for everyone – rich in nature and a real recreational draw, it's also steeped in history.

This diverse woodland, close to the centre of Falkirk, features ancient oak woodland and more recent conifer plantation. Visitors are well catered for with a museum, playpark, golf course and loch in adjacent Callendar Park, while tranquil spots are still plentiful. A good network of surfaced paths serves the wood, which is very popular with dog walkers and a haven for wildlife.

Callendar Wood
© Colin McCulloch

Carron Glen
Denny
(NS785835) 19 ha (46 acres) SSSI
Scottish Wildlife Trust

Tranquil, peaceful and different from all other woodlands in the Falkirk area, Carron Glen is a semi-natural broadleaved woodland with a sense of wildness about it.

Served by narrow, undulating and often muddy paths, the wood lines the steep north bank of the River Carron, where dippers can be spotted along with otters and kingfishers.

In spring and summer the site is alive with wildflowers and it's rich in woodland birds.

Muiravonside Country Park
Linlithgow
(NS960756) 61 ha (170 acres)
Falkirk Council

Eighty species of birds plus foxes, roe deer, grey squirrels, rabbits, badgers, bats and great crested newt are all residents at Muiravonside Country Park.

The site has a visitor centre, a rare breeds farm, and a programme of organised events, though families can also enjoy peaceful, quiet woodland walks. The site has a rich variety of wildlife habitats, including a mixed woodland, wildflower meadow and wildlife ponds. The River Avon Heritage Trail also passes along the site's boundary.

Other woods in the Falkirk area include Roughcastle Community Woodland, (NS845797), a small area of woodland adjacent to the Roman Antonine Wall, which is an important but fragile archaeological site, and Kilbean Wood (NS875780) part of the Callendar Estates but managed by the Lionthorn Community Woodland Group.

Muiravonside Country Park
© Colin McCulloch

Renfrewshire

Gleniffer Braes Country Park

Paisley

(NS456606) 480 ha (1,186 acres)

Renfrewshire Council

Woodland walks, spectacular views, open moorland, grassland, heath, scrub, streams and waterfalls – and ample family activities – are all part of the make up of massive Gleniffer Braes Country Park.

Wild, yet tranquil, the site is dominated by broadleaved plantations, with younger conifer areas and plenty of routes to walk. Large sections of the park are important locally for natural heritage. Ancient woodland plants, such as dog's mercury and sweet woodruff, abound in the Glen Park area.

Most of the woodland lies to the east and is best approached from Glen Park, which features an outstanding 11 metre (35 ft) waterfall and offers some wonderful views. Bluebells feature in spring and there are ponds and a good range of woodland birds, especially in spring and summer.

From cairns to quarries, history is never far away – Second World War bomb craters and gun placements can still be seen west of Robertson Park.

Clyde Muirshiel Regional Park
Largs, Greenock and Lochwinnoch
(NS312632) 28,100 ha (69,435 acres) 6 SSSIs
Private but visitor facilities managed by local authority
www.clydemuirshiel.co.uk

Clyde Muirshiel Regional Park is a haven for recreation and wildlife alike. A rural idyll on the urban fringe, the park has many mature woods, open moorland, an old volcanic plug, marshes, waterfalls ponds and streams. It contains a number of notable woodland areas, which span across three different unitary areas; Renfrewshire, Inverclyde and North Ayrshire.

These include:

Muirshiel Country Park
Calder Glen, Lochwinnoch
(NS313632) 29 ha (73 acres)
Renfrewshire Council

Once a Victorian shooting estate, in the 1960s Muirshiel Country Park was established as a sitka plantation, but is now being managed as a variety of woodland habitats containing pine, birch, alder and oak. A well-maintained trail leads onto the moorland and to Windy Hill, where there are scenic views of Ben Lomond, while sightings of wildlife, such as skylark and hen harrier are also likely.

Muirshiel Country Park
© Clyde Muirshiel Regional Park

Parkhill Wood
Castle Semple Country Park, Lochwinnoch
(NS367599) 28 ha (70 acres)
Renfrewshire Council

Parkhill Wood (NS358591) was planted nearly 200 years ago as part of a designed landscape. A peaceful haven with centuries-old yews, fishponds and a grotto, it's also home to pipistrelle bats, great spotted woodpecker and roe deer.

The scenic Shielhill Glen nearby (see below), is also part of the Clyde Muirshiel Regional Park. It has a visitor centre and a popular nature trail, and offers fantastic views across the Clyde and Cowal peninsular.

Parkhill Wood
© Carol Crawford

Inverclyde

Shielhill Glen Wood
Inverkip
(NS247721) 6 ha (15 acres) SSSI
**Privately owned by the
Ardgowan Estate**

Shielhill Glen Wood is part of a complex of woods which represent the best mixed deciduous woodland in Inverclyde. Just three miles from town, it has the feel of somewhere remote, yet is well served by paths and trails. The site includes the Shielhill Glen Nature Trail which is managed by the rangers of the Clyde Muirshiel Regional Park (see above).

There's a wide range of native trees, including oak, ash, rowan and birch, and a combination of open and wooded habitats. A good range of flora and fungi, woodland and moorland birds and striking views across the glen all add to the experience.

Shielhill Glen Wood

© Carol Crawford

Midlothian

Roslin Glen
Penicuik, Loanhead
(NT275625) 18 ha (45 acres) SSSI
Scottish Wildlife Trust

Adventurous visitors keen to enjoy a gorge woodland should visit Roslin Glen, the largest and most diverse remaining example of an ancient wood in Midlothian. Lying to the south side of the North Esk river, the terrain is very steep and access is via muddy paths, so the site isn't suited to family outings.

However, those who are able to tackle the terrain can enjoy some of the 200 different species of flowering plant to be found in the glen. Generally at its best in spring – it includes great woodrush, wood sorrel, dog's mercury, ramsons and golden saxifrage, plus a number of species rare to Scotland, including rough horsetail and wood melick.

Roe deer and badgers might also be glimpsed in the wood, together with 60 different species of breeding birds – including woodpeckers.

Part of the Crown Estate, the site is leased to, and managed by, the Scottish Wildlife Trust and lies immediately adjacent to the Roslin Glen Country Park (NT333620) managed by Midlothian Council – also worth a look.

Other attractions to visit while in the area include the Rosslyn Chapel and Rosslyn Castle, both of which reside on the north bank of the Esk River immediately opposite the wildlife reserve and adjacent to the country park.

Roslin Glen
© Margaret Thorne

© Margaret Thorne

Vogrie

Vogrie
Dalkeith
(NT380633) 104 ha (257 acres)
Midlothian Council

Worth a visit if you're in the area, Vogrie is a Victorian parkland estate with woodland walks, meadows, rolling parkland and an original walled garden. The focal point is the baronial style Vogrie House, with beautiful landscaped vistas.

Choose from three suggested walking routes, along flat, well-maintained paths and enjoy some magnificent specimen trees, vibrant ground flora and a range of woodland birds. There are three ponds – and the River Tyne also flows through the site.

Currie Wood
Borthwick

(NT374593) 21 ha (53 acres)
Woodland Trust Scotland

A real hidden gem, not to be missed while in the area, Currie Wood is a petite ancient woodland with a mix of broadleaves and planted conifers. It's set in the steep gorge of Middleton South Burn above Borthwick Castle. The latter, now a luxury hotel, once provided refuge for Mary Queen of Scots.

Though only a relatively small site, it would make a fantastic location for a mediaeval film set. For example, visitors can sit under a gnarled old pine tree and not see anything around except woodland, despite the fact that the site is within spitting distance of Edinburgh.

A circular footpath leads visitors through its fantastic walks, among ancient oak, birch, Scots pine, and ash woodland, and provides impressive views of the sandstone cliffs, the ravine and the burn below.

Woodland Trust Scotland is in the process of restoring the conifer plantation in Currie Wood, to benefit both people and wildlife. The site includes 53 different moss species and 105 plants have been found on site, such as moschatel, greater pond-sedge, wood crane's bill and oak fern, the latter of which is relatively uncommon.

Currie Wood
© WTPL/Pat Herbert

West Lothian

Beecraigs Country Park
Linlithgow
(NS998737) 370 ha (913 acres)
West Lothian Council

Beecraigs Country Park nestles high in the Bathgate Hills. There's something for everyone here; visitors can enjoy anything from peaceful walks to trout fishing, riding to archery.

There's also the chance to spot a red squirrel, roe deer and a host of birds among the dense, mixed woodland that's criss-crossed by streams and features two ponds and a red deer farm.

Beecraigs Country Park
© Alan Melrose

A good network of surfaced paths and forest roads give excellent access to the host of attractions and there are three colour-coded waymarked trails to help with exploration – all of them easy routes.

A short, steep walk to the top of the privately owned Cockleroy Hill (just outside the park) is rewarded with panoramic views of the Forth and Lothians.

Just to the south-west of Beecraigs is the privately owned Witchcraig Wood (NS988727), which is a mixed woodland on the upper slopes of a hillside.

There is a short, steepish climb to the summit but, as well as impressive views of the Forth Valley, at the top you'll also find a Refuge Stone and a wall containing 43 different rocks to illustrate the geological diversity of the area.

Other sites within easy distance of Beecraigs include Almondell and Calderwood Country Park (NT091685) described as 'the best kept secret in West Lothian' and Polkemmet Country Park (NS924649) both managed by West Lothian Council.

Bellsquarry Wood
Livingston
(NT048650) 17 ha (43 acres)
Woodland Trust Scotland

Unusually rich in all kinds of wildlife, Bellsquarry Wood is a popular urban walk.

The wood combines semi-natural regenerated birch, with a mature broadleaf area of oak and beech trees, and a few scattered Scots pines. There is a pond and the Dedridge burn, which runs east through grassland, both adding an aquatic element to the mix.

This diverse range of habitats sustains bryophytes, invertebrates, fungi, a variety of birds and many small mammals.

There are plenty of pleasant walks, and not far away is another Woodland Trust Scotland site, Blaeberry Wood (NS958646). Near Whitburn, it is set between two communities, with two burns running through it. Served by a good network of paths, it can be enjoyed by walkers, riders and cyclists alike.

East Lothian

Woodhall Dean
Dunbar
(NT681728) 60 ha (148 acres) SSSI
Scottish Wildlife Trust

Woodhall Dean lines the narrow branching valleys of the Woodhall, Weatherly and Boonslie Burns and incorporates the largest remaining area of sessile oak wood in East Lothian.

Relatively undisturbed, secluded and peaceful, with wonderfully varied habitats, it is

Woodhall Dean
© Margaret Thorne

dominated by oak, but also contains hazel, aspen, holly, elm and wild cherry. It boasts a rich, lush shrub layer, with a colourful ground cover of bluebells, primroses, wood sage, red campion and dog's mercury.

Sparrowhawks, buzzards, tawny owls and great spotted woodpeckers are among a rich bird population that can be glimpsed year-round. It also has some magnificent veteran cliff-top oaks with roots visibly gripping the narrow fissures of the bedrock. There are some good views from the path at the head of the gorge out to the countryside and sea beyond.

Pressmennan
Dunbar
(NT630729) 86 ha (212 acres)
Woodland Trust Scotland

Pressmennan Wood is situated next to the village of Stenton, five miles southwest of Dunbar. It is one of the last traces of the ancient native woodland that once covered the south-east of Scotland. It is a fantastic place to visit, with panoramic views, impressive ancient oaks along the shores of Pressmennan Lake and an abundance of wildlife.

Along the footpaths many plants can be seen including wood sorrel, wood anemone, honeysuckle and in spring, primrose and bluebell. Woodland birds such as chaffinch, great and coal tit, goldcrest, chiffchaff and willow warbler are common. The yellowhammer can also be spotted along the woodland edge. Bennet's Burn together with the lake, also provides habitats for otters and other wetland wildlife.

Part of the original oak wood is intact. However, the bulk of it was felled and replanted with conifers in the 1950s. It is now in the process of being gradually restored to native species by the Woodland Trust Scotland.

Butterdean Wood
Gladsmuir, Haddington
(NT456721) 42 ha (104 acres)
Woodland Trust Scotland and East Lothian Council

The story goes that in 1649, Isabel and Margaret Bartilman met the devil and danced with him at 'Butterdam', which is the earliest known mention of Butterdean Wood.

This wood has had a mixed history, having been felled and regenerated several times since being first planted in the early 1700s. Today, it is best described as a mixed wood, as it veers from conifer through to mixed woodland and then onto pure broadleaves, with a scattering of veteran trees throughout.

Providing cover for foxes and roe deer, it supports a wealth of other wildlife; birds like chiffchaff, wren, goldcrest, long-tailed tit and willow warbler, plus plants such as wood sorrel, honeysuckle, primrose and the notable bird's nest orchid.

Two waymarked paths take visitors through its variety of woodland habitats and, being one of the larger woodland areas in the district, it can be enjoyed by foot, cycle or horse.

But come prepared because it can get quite muddy in winter.

Newhailes Woodland
Musselburgh
(NT327725) 44 ha (86 acres)
National Trust for Scotland

Newhailes Woodland, part of a large parkland estate and designed landscape, surrounds a magnificent, historic house within the heart of an urban area.

The woodland covers around a third of the site and was the location of the first evergreen oak planted in Scotland. It provides a quiet and peaceful setting for recreation. Look out for the 18th-century shell grotto, water garden and teahouse.

The nearby Inveresk Lodge Garden Woodland (NT348716), also owned by the National Trust for Scotland, was created to provide shelter for Inveresk House. A peaceful one-acre woodland, it offers pleasant walks with some large and interesting feature trees.

Explore it as part of a woodland trail with the garden and you'll enjoy the sights and sounds of wild birds, hedgehogs, foxes, goldfinches and kestrels.

However, please note that, unlike Newhailes, dogs are not permitted at Inveresk and the paths are less suitable for wheelchair users.

Newhailes Woodland
© Margaret Thorne

Yellowcraig
Dirleton
(NT518856) 14 ha (35 acres) SSSI
East Lothian Council

Set by a long, sweeping, sandy beach with views across the sea to the island of Fidra, Yellowcraig is part of a beautiful landscape with a rich ecological mix.

It's ideal for family days out with rock pools, an adventure playground and the chance to enjoy a cool, shady walk through the sheltered woodland, containing an interesting selection of ground flora and fungi.

Interest is added by some huge beeches within the wood itself and on the seaward edge, some ancient windblown larch and Scots pine trees.

Yellowcraig
© Margaret Thorne

81

WESTERN HIGHLANDS

© Peter Quelch

Carradale Forest

This is where it all starts to get really wild. Mountains and lochs begin to pose dramatic backdrops for many of the woods, parks and gardens. Big trees sit in big settings, perhaps few bigger than the monsters at Ardkinglass Woodland Garden.

Once again, within the broadleaf woods, there is evidence of an industrial past with oaks in particular – once coppiced for charcoal to fire iron furnaces.

Exploring several sites around Loch Lomond alone gives a rich and varied introduction to the delights of the Western Highlands. Beautiful alpine flora is to be found on Ben Lomond (Scotland's southern most 'Munro'), perhaps even a glimpse of red deer or mountain hare, whilst the loch is surrounded by bird rich wetlands and fine oak woods; and all this just a short hop from the hustle and bustle of Glasgow.

ARCHIE MILES

Map
no.

See map overleaf for wood locations ▸▸

MAP 5 - WESTERN HIGHLANDS

The above map is a guide only. Please contact relevant organisations for more detailed location information.

85

Stirling

Glen Finglas
Callander
(NN521108) 4,000 ha (10,000 acres) SSSI, NP
Woodland Trust Scotland
www.glen-finglas.info

Offering magnificent, expansive views, the beautiful estate of Glen Finglas has been an important part of Stirling's landscape for thousands of years. Once the most popular of all royal hunting forests, it now forms part of the Loch Lomond and Trossachs National Park and is the Woodland Trust Scotland's largest site.

Three glens, divided by mountain ridges, radiate from the heart of this extensive estate – the western valley is called Glen Finglas, the central one, Gleann nam Meann and the eastern one is Gleann Casaig – all of which retain fragments of woodland and isolated trees.

In fact, Glen Finglas is believed by woodland

Glen Finglas

© WTPL/John McKinlay

historians to feature one of the largest collection of ancient trees in Scotland. Hundreds of its veteran trees can be enjoyed from the many trails created for visitors to explore this exciting site.

A stroll from one of the two car parks will take you through beautiful woodland of oak and birch, across heather, wood pasture, and shapely hills. Seasoned hill walkers and mountain bikers can enjoy the ambitious route up the two Corbetts, Ben Vane and Ben Ledi, or the Mell Trail, while less-ambitious visitors may prefer to follow the shorter stroll along the surfaced path around Little Drum Wood. Whatever your preference

there are options from 15 minutes to 15 miles.

Above all, Glen Finglas is a landscape with a sense of tranquillity and history about it. Sir Walter Scott was inspired by this site, writing about it in his epic poem, *The Lady of the Lake* and his ballad, *Glenfinlas,* a lament about a fatal hunting expedition. Rob Roy is also closely linked with this landscape – it is likely he travelled through Glen Finglas on some of his historic journeys.

Today, slightly less famous visitors follow in his footsteps, including staff from the Woodland Trust Scotland, who are engaged in a major programme to protect and restore this ancient woodland landscape.

Queen Elizabeth Forest Park
Cowal & Trossachs

(NN522014) 20,240 ha (50,000 acres) SSSI, NSA, NP

Forestry Commission Scotland

The attractions of the vast Queen Elizabeth Forest Park, also part of the Loch Lomond and Trossach's National Park,

extend almost as far as the site itself, with mountains, moors, forests, rivers, waterfalls and lochs to explore and discover.

Tranquil woodland, fantastic views over the Trossachs and a treasure trove of visitor activities ensure that all needs are met in this delightful forest park, which was designated in 1953 to commemorate the coronation of Queen Elizabeth II. ▸▸

The site extends from the eastern shore of Loch Lomond to Strathyre Forest Park, with a wonderful variety of habitats and a rich wildlife population – everything from red and roe deer to grouse and red squirrels.

A number of different woodland areas exist within the park and, although the trees have been mainly planted, there are still some remnants of ancient woodland.

One of these is Callander Crags (NN630085). Situated on south-facing slopes, it's a steep climb to the summit above the treeline, but you're rewarded by fantastic views and can continue from here onto Bracklinn Falls.

The David Marshall Lodge Visitor Centre (NN520014), which lies at the heart of the park, is a good starting point for exploring the many routes and trails, from wide gravel-surfaced forest tracks to woodland paths and steep trails. In short, there is something for everyone.

Callander Crags
© Colin McCulloch

Craigrostan Woodlands
Aberfoyle
(NN342074) 124 ha (306 acres)
SSSI, NP

**The Jenson Foundation and
Scottish Woodlands**

Natural regeneration of native trees is being actively encouraged to expand this ancient oak woodland, which adorns the steeply sloping eastern shore of Loch Lomond within the National Park. Higher up, the ancient trees give way to a mosaic of coniferous plantation and hillside heath. A path, which is steep in parts, leads through both areas of woodland, offering a detour to Rob Roy's view, with some grand views of the loch and surrounding landscape.

Roe deer, red deer, wild goats and the occasional golden eagle have been recorded on the site, along with pine martens and pied flycatcher.

Venture within the woodland and you might also happen across the remnants of a 17th-century village.

Another nearby site well worth a visit is Inversnaid (NN335105) which lies on steep rocky slopes above the loch. This site is also being managed by the RSPB to encourage natural regeneration of the mature broadleaved woodland. There are two paths through the wood – the West Highland Way and the Nature Trail, from both of which there are good views across the loch on clear days.

Craigrostan Woodlands
© Lewis Mullen

89

Ben Lomond
Rowardennan, by Drymen
(NS359987) 35 ha (86 acres)
SSSI, NP
National Trust for Scotland

Dominating the landscape as it rises out of the eastern shore of Loch Lomond to an imposing height of more than 915 metres (3,000 ft), Ben Lomond – the 'beacon hill'– is a mosaic of steep oak woodland, rough grassland and plantation, with open heath and grassland. Vibrant woodland flowers bring colour to the site in spring, while in summer, butterflies abound.

The woodland was planted in the late 18th century, when its timber was used as fuel for iron smelting, signs of which can still be discovered today.

The broadleaved areas, accessed from the Ardess Hidden History Trail (NS361992), feature mature planted oaks with holly and hazel, and higher up regenerating birch, aspen and rowan. The main hill path, leading to the summit, ascends steeply through a coniferous plantation.

Nearby, on the road between Balmaha and Rowardenanna, you'll also find Cashel – The Forest for a Thousand Years (NS400940). Managed by the Royal Scottish Forestry Society, this 1,230 hectare (340 acre) site situated on Cashel Farm was planted, over the last 10 years, as a working forest to replicate the natural changes in upland vegetation and tree species. Its Native Forest Centre provides information and displays and there are three waymarked trails. For further details visit: www.cashel.org.uk

Ben Lomond
© Colin McCulloch

Plean Country Park
Plean
(NS829866) 81 ha (200 acres)
Stirling Council

The creation of a rich mosaic of thriving wildlife habitats has transformed Plean Country Park from its once derelict landscape (following the closure many years earlier of an open cast mining operation on site). It now consists of a diverse range of habitats including broadleaf and mixed woodland, with birch, oak, Scots pine species, a wildflower meadow, damp shaded areas (carpeted with mosses and heathers, lichens and fungi) and a pond. A burn also flows through the park and an extensive path network provide a variety of waymarked routes and trails, catering for all interests and abilities.

About 48 km (30 miles) away is another Stirling Council site – Mugdock Country Park (NS550778) near Milngavie. This 260 hectare (642 acre) site, also managed by East Dunbartonshire Council, is considered special for its variety of different habitats, including Mugdock Wood, an area of ancient broadleaved woodland. It's a peaceful, tranquil wood, with the sense of a place lost in time.

Plean Country Park
© Colin McCulloch

Argyll & Bute

Taynish
Tayvallich
(NR737852) 330 ha (815 acres)
NNR
Scottish Natural Heritage

One of Scotland's finest nature reserves, oak trees have been flourishing at Taynish for 6000 years or more, a little longer than people have lived there. In the past, these trees would have been a source of timber and charcoal but they now form part of one of Britain's largest remaining native oakwoods – hence Taynish's status as a National Nature Reserve.

The Woodland Trail, a 5 km (3 mile) circular route leads you into the heart of this 'northern rainforest' – so called because of its damp conditions. Situated on a hidden peninsula between Linne Mhuirich and Loch Sween, it has a mixture of shoreline, grassland, scrub, bog, heath and woodland habitats.

Mosses, liverworts and lichens grow wonderfully well in these humid conditions and you'll see hay-scented buckler and other ferns everywhere.

Listen out quietly for the trills and warning calls of wood warblers in spring, while buzzards and woodpeckers may also be spotted at other times of year, along with tawny owls who come out at dusk.

Insects and other invertebrates also thrive, including 13 species of dragonfly and 20 species of butterfly, all dashing about in the waterloggoed mires.

The coastal path takes you through flower-rich grasslands, home to the rare marsh fritillary butterfly, while the rapids at the end of the coastal path are rich in sea life, such as wading birds and otters – if you're lucky you might spot one of the latter out fishing.

Reasonably fit, energetic walkers might like to take the trail up to Barr Mor. It is slightly steep but you can enjoy great views from the bench at the top. There is also an easier, wheelchair-accessible route to the former grain mill ruin. Either way, remember to wear strong, waterproof footwear and clothing.

A trip to Taynish could be combined with Barnluasgan in Knapdale (see below) or Crinan Wood (see below) at the west end of the Crinan Canal – both offer splendid views over Knapdale, Moine Mhor and the Sound of Jura.

Loch Coille Bharr
Lochgilphead
(NR783903) Within Knapdale Forest 5,734 ha (14,000 acres) SSSI
Forestry Commission Scotland

The woodlands of Loch Coille Bharr, which lie on low, rocky hills, are part of an extensive reserve which take in the Knapdale Habitats Partnership Reserve, the Faery Isles and Barnluasgan.

The Loch Coille Barr reserve is a popular recreation area that's also rich in archaeological interest. Much of the reserve is carpeted with rare mosses, ferns and lichens. A delightful 5 km (3 mile) trail from the centre of the Knapdale Forest circuits Loch Coille Bharr, via a series of quiet and little-used forest tracks.

Always peaceful and teeming with wildlife, the walk leads ▸▸

Loch Coille Bharr
© Peter Quelch

through remnant native woods which circle the inland loch. Itself an ever-changing and beautiful part of the landscape, the wood features a pretty old mill stream, a host of old oaks and the chance to spot roe deer, wildfowl and wood ant nests.

Moving on beyond the Loch Coille Barr walk, you'll find Barnluasgan (NR790909), the access point for some very special walks in the Knapdale Forest (including a very attractive oakwood trail through its centre). It contains large areas of semi-natural oakwood and regenerating mixed native broadleaved woodland, while it's noted for its oceanic lichens (which feature oak, ash, hazel and willow trees) and also for being a rich bat habitat.

Alternatively, you can get to the heart of the Faery Isles, which feature extensive areas of delightful ancient semi-natural oakwoods as well as planted forests with old spruce, Scots pines and Douglas fir, adding a majestic touch to the scene. The forest tracks provide good long walks to some of the most delightful parts of these uniquely beautiful coastal forests, or you can take a small boat or canoe out onto the water for the best chance to really appreciate the beauty of the Faery Isles.

Crinan Wood
Crinan, near Lochgilphead
(NR788943) 30 ha (75 acres) NSA
Woodland Trust Scotland

Just half a day is enough to enjoy a full tour of Crinan, adjacent to the larger forest of Knapdale, and take full advantage of its unique position atop a prominent rocky knoll with magnificent views to Jura, the Corryvreckan and Mull.

Bringing together sea, sand and woodland, Crinan Wood is a place of echoes – in the past royalty, priests, farmers, soldiers, sailors, and even Celtic settlers from more than 1500 years ago, would have all passed through or near this wood.

Ever-changing scenery and temperate rainforest conditions are created by its climate of warm air, sea mist, drizzle and

© Peter Quelch

Crinan Wood

downpour. These are perfect for the wealth of mosses, ferns, lichens and fungi which thrive here. The bird species include wood warbler, redstarts, tree pipit, pied flycatcher, heron and buzzard – many of which can be heard to combine in a blend of birdsong. Red deer and otters are just some of the other discoveries to be made by the more observant visitor.

It's served by clear, well waymarked paths that are easy to follow, with a few steep bits that aren't too challenging, past some wonderful old gnarled oaks that have been moulded by winds, and lichen-covered hazels, which bring to life its ancient heritage.

95

© Peter Quelch

Minard Woodland

Minard Woodland
Minard, near Lochgilphead
(NR978962) 170 ha (420 acres)
Forestry Commission Scotland
and various private owners

More than 100 bird species have been spotted in the well-loved and delightful mature woods of Minard Castle, a mix of oakwood and planted conifers with beautiful old beech and lime trees, huge goat willows and some very old oaks.

The woodland is full of character and its heritage trail leads along a delightful shoreline before climbing up to a viewpoint that provides fantastic views of the coastline.

Ardcastle Wood
Lochgair village, near Lochgilphead
(NR942920) 400 ha (988 acres)
Forestry Commission Scotland

Serene and pretty Ardcastle Wood, part of the much older Kilmichael Forest, is a great place to head for long, energetic walks and the chance to admire some magnificent mature conifers.

The site, inhabited both by woodland and sea birds, contains lots of popular forest walks of various lengths – many of them leading to the beautiful, unspoiled shores of Loch Fyne.

Ardcastle Wood

© Peter Quelch

97

Achnabreck
Lochgilphead
(NR852908) Within Kilmichael
forest 7,721 ha (19,000 acres)
Forestry Commission Scotland

Great for picnics, walks and
some ambitious cycling, the
cup and ring-marked stones at
Achnabreck and the oak-
wooded hill fort of Dun na
Maraig form a scenic corner of
the huge Kilmichael Forest.

The site boasts some good,
firm, well-made paths and the
views across Loch Fyne from
these Scheduled Ancient
Monuments are excellent and
very well interpreted.

Achnabreck
© Peter Quelch

Dun Na Cuaiche
Inveraray
(NN095093) 14 ha (35 acres)
Privately owned
www.inveraray-castle.com

A steep, wooded hill
overlooking Inveraray Castle,
Dun Na Cuaiche has a
network of paths that offer
walks through a wide variety
of woodland types and ages.

A world away from the
bustling town and castle below,
the wood is full of interesting
trees, both native and planted,
rich in ground flora, and full of
ruins and features associated
with the castle's past.

Nearby, you'll also find
Balantyre Wood (NN087115)
which is part of the Argyll
Estates and lies within the
grounds of Inveraray Castle, the
latter being home to the Duke
of Argyll.

Ardkinglas Woodland Garden
Cairndow nr. Inveraray
(NN179106) 10 ha (25 acres)
Privately owned
www.ardkinglas.com

Some of the tallest conifers in Britain feature among a host of other large and important trees within this mature woodland garden and arboretum.

The peaceful setting, with its historic garden and small lochan, is well worth a visit to view some of the rare specimens that stand out among the silver firs, spruces and rhododendrons.

Ardkinglas Woodland Garden
© Bob Black

Leacann Muir Forest Drive

Inveraray

(NN029031) and (NM934062)

20 km (12.5 miles)

Forestry Commission Scotland

Launched in April 2007, this massive and remote forest drive allows you to travel by car across the Eredine Forest, through terrain that few people will ever have seen before.

However, it is not for the fainthearted, as it crosses remote and previously untamed territory some 305 metres (1,000 ft) above sea level.

But, not surprisingly, the views from this exciting new forest drive, through previously inaccessible moors and spruce forest lying between Loch Fyne and Loch Awe, are breathtakingly magnificent and rewarding.

Leacann Muir Forest Drive

© Peter Quelch

© Peter Quelch

Beinn Ghuilean Forest

Beinn Ghuilean Forest
Campbeltown
(NR711195) 200 ha (494 acres)
Forestry Commission Scotland

It's worth the climb through the young, attractive larch-filled woodland of Beinn Ghuilean for the unique vista across Campbeltown, its harbour, loch and the Davaar Island.

Buzzards, kestrels, wildfowl and a dense covering of butterworts are just some of the rich cocktail of wildlife thriving in this wet environment. From here, it's easy to get to Kildonan Dun, a spectacular Scheduled Ancient Monument on the shore overlooking Arran.

Carradale Forest
Carradale
(NR800382) 833 ha (2,058 acres)
Forestry Commission Scotland

Tucked away close to the once-busy fishing village of Carradale, this extensive forest is never far from the sea. It nestles between the Carradale and Arran coasts, where you might also spot the odd basking shark!

A new long-distance footpath, the Kintyre Way, passes through Carradale and from this, it's worth a detour inside the forest for the chance to enjoy some wonderful views from the summit of Cnoc na Gabhar, on the Deer Hill walk, across to the mountains of Arran.

Carradale Forest

© Peter Quelch

© Bob Black

Glen Nant

Glen Nant

Taynuilt
(NN020272) 332 ha (820 acres)
SSSI, NNR
Forestry Commission Scotland

Rich in wildlife, this large site including ancient oakwoods by the River Nant, can be explored via a range of waymarked trails, which allow visitors the chance to enjoy nature and history simultaneously.

Glen Nant was once a centre for the charcoal industry and the woodland bears evidence of this in its coppiced oak trees, numerous charcoal platforms and a reconstructed charcoal kiln.

There is a short all–ability path along the riverside leading to a picnic spot. The Ant Trail, a longer path named after the wood ants living in the forest, takes visitors through the wood, but unfortunately its not really suitable for less-able visitors.

Some of the views from the wood are truly delightful, offering vistas across the glen and the neighbouring mountains. The reserve includes an extensive area of harvested conifer plantation, currently being converted to native woodland.

A visit to this wood could be combined with a visit to Dalavich Oakwood, the Bonawe Iron Furnace and the Inverawe Smokehouses nearby.

Glasdrum Wood
Appin
(NN001454) 169 ha (418 acres)
SSSI, NNR
Scottish Natural Heritage

This tranquil ancient woodland is internationally important for its mosses and lichens and the abundance of butterflies it supports, among them the chequered skipper and pearl-bordered fritillary. Red and roe deer can also be found on the site, along with red squirrels and pine martens.

The wood lines the steep slopes on the banks above upper Loch Creran and includes a variety of native trees and shrubs. Ancient oaks and ash trees dominate the site which is, in fact, part of a larger complex of native woodland stretching up Glen Creran and down the loch as far as the Creagan Bridge.

There's a rich history associated with the place, which at one time was used commercially to supply charcoal for the Bonawe Iron Foundry.

Visitors can enjoy the wood from a waymarked trail, though conditions can be challenging in other steeper sections of the site.

A trip to Glasdrum could be combined with one to Sutherland Grove (NM966422) just 8 km (5 miles) away. Named after Lord Sutherland, this Forestry Commission Scotland site consists of a grove of majestic Douglas firs by the Abhinn Teithil Burn and a variety of waymarked trails into Barcaldine Forest, where a number of rare invertebrates have been recorded The path along the wooded ravine above the grove is particularly atmospheric.

Ballachuan Hazel Wood
Oban
(NM763156) 49 ha (121 acres)
Scottish Wildlife Trust

If you're interested in wildlife, Ballachuan Hazel Wood should feature high on your list of 'must see' destinations because it ranks among the country's best examples of coastal Atlantic hazelwood and is recognised as being of international importance for its treasure trove of lichen species.

Herons, otters, roe deer and marsh fritillary butterflies can all be found in the wood, which is served by a network of occasionally challenging paths.

And, on top of all that, its position on the western edge of Argyll affords outstanding views of nearby Hebridean islands.

Some of the hazel trees on site are really ancient and there are small stands of mature beech trees which have great character.

For those interested in heritage, the site also contains the ruins of an ancient settlement and nearby, Easdale Island, once a centre for local slate quarrying, is full of industrial archaeological interest too.

Aros Park
Tobermory, Isle of Mull
(NM516540) 200 ha (495 acres)
SSSI
Forestry Commission Scotland

Aros Park
© Forestry Commission Scotland

The coastal views from the popular yet peaceful woodland of Aros Park are, in short, 'outstanding'.

The woods stretch around the edge of Tobermory Bay into the town of Tobermory itself and incorporate some excellent, tranquil walks and a good range of facilities for visitors. This is a good example of west coast downy woodland and, although large trees are scarce, there is an area of mature native oakwood near a central lochan.

Puck's Glen
Dunoon
(NS148844) Within the Argyll
Forest Park 20,000 ha
(50,000 acres)
Forestry Commission Scotland

Once part of the Younger
family's Benmore Estate, Puck's
Glen is now just one of the
many woodland areas within
the much larger Argyll Forest
Park, but is notable because it
forms part of one of the most
famous walks on the Cowal
Peninsula.

A steep but well-made path,
originally created by the
Younger family in the late 19th
century, leads uphill to a folly
and onto the Younger Botanic
Garden. You can also do the Big
Tree Walk from Puck's Glen.
This takes you past some very
impressive Californian
redwoods and Douglas firs.

The Ardgarton Visitor Centre,
within Argyll Forest Park,
provides information on other
walks and cycle routes, such as
Cruach Tairbeirt (NN312045),
part of the Tarbet Loop.

Also worth a visit is the
nearby Bishop's Glen, managed
by the Argyll and Bute
Council, set in the heart of
Dunoon Woodland Park
(NS165766). This mixed
woodland has excellent views
over Dunoon and across the
Clyde.

Puck's Glen

© Bob Black

GRAMPIANS

Here you are in the Queen's Country – many of the woods and estates have names which have entered the national vernacular only because they surround the royal retreat at Balmoral. This is also the land of the Dee and the Spey, the two great rivers which once floated the timbers down from the great pine forests to the coast in the 18th and 19th centuries.

Scots pines, and some of the biggest specimens in Scotland at that, along with birch, hold sway along these great river valleys. This is also the best part of Scotland to discover aspen, that Cinderella of native Scottish trees. Visit this region in autumn to revel in the burnished gold of the turning birches and aspens.

You can head into the mountains for a truly remote ramble or follow the well-worn tracks and trails through fine estates and country parks.

ARCHIE MILES

See map overleaf for wood locations ▸▸

MAP 6 - GRAMPIANS

Please refer to page 107 for wood names and details of further information.

The above map is a guide only. Please contact relevant organisations for more detailed location information.

109

Aberdeenshire

Glen Tanar
Aboyne
(NO480966) 10,000 ha (25,000 acres) SSSI, NNR
Privately owned
www.glentanar.co.uk

You're guaranteed stunning scenery, space and peace on a visit to Glen Tanar, an ancient Caledonian pine forest, dotted with streams and burns, that lies on Royal Deeside.

This vast estate has pleasures in store for any family, whether it's taking a leisurely stroll along the pinewood trails,

fishing for salmon in the river or trout in the loch, or picnicking by the burn.

Among the pinewoods there are some very old Caledonian pines, some believed to date back between 300 and 400 years. There are also areas of commercial woodland, with a variety of native trees added to the mix, along the riverbanks on the lower areas of the estate.

Higher up, the woods lead onto open areas of heather moorland and it's from here that you can appreciate the full impact of the fabulous views across the estate and the eastern Cairngorms.

Buzzards, eagles, the rare capercaillie and a host of native woodland birds are resident on the estate, along with roe and red deer, otters and a large number of different plant species.

There's a network of waymarked trails radiating from the centre, providing a choice of scenic walks that will suit all abilities. It's possible to follow the higher walks right out on

Glen Tanar
© Alan Melrose

to the hill and to the easternmost Munro.

Those with time to spare can combine their visit with a trip to Aboyne Castle and Coo Cathedral in nearby Aboyne, where there's also a nice area of community woodland – Bell Wood – that offers views across the village and surrounding hills.

Muir of Dinnet
Aboyne
(NO429998) 1160 ha (2866 acres)
SSSI, NNR, NP
Scottish Natural Heritage

Extensive birchwood, heather moor, wetlands and two large lochs make up the breathtakingly beautiful Muir of Dinnet. Steeped in history, the site is linked to a host of interesting cultural, historical and archaeological stories, just some of the reasons that make this a special site to visit and enjoy.

The wood, which is situated on low-lying ground, is home to a number of relatively rare species, most particularly the pearl-bordered fritillary butterfly; while out on the moor Scottish crossbill, Cladonia lichen and aspen bristle moss can be found.

Apart from the two lochs, Kinord and Davan, which attract breeding and wintering wildfowl, there is a clutch of small burns on the estate, including Vat Burn which is a real beauty spot on an already stunning landscape.

Forest trails connect the Muir of Dinnet with Cambus O' May, which is part of the upper Deeside Forests managed by the Forestry Commission.

You'll also find Balmoral Castle not far away.

Muir of Dinnet
© Alan Melrose

Craigendarroch Oakwood
© Alan Melrose

Craigendarroch Oakwood
Ballater
(NO365975) Within the Invercauld Estate 43,600 ha (107,700 acres) SSSI
Privately owned by the Invercauld Estate
www.invercauld.org

There is something special about Craigendarroch – the 'hill of oaks' – one of the largest and highest oakwoods in the north east of Scotland. A rare oak wood locally, this historic site, formerly managed as oak coppice for the production of tan bark and spoke wood, was once part of the Royal Burgh of Ballater and retains a royal link today. It lies on the Invercauld Estate in the heart of the Cairngorms National Park – also known as Royal Deeside.

A climb through the wood, as the path gradually rises upwards, soon reveals evidence of the planted nature of the site. The paths on the lower slopes are well-managed but care is needed as you get higher, since the paths become rougher and steeper. As you get higher, the oaks begin to thin to make way for birch and Scots pine which dominate the higher ground.

Once you reach the 402 metre (1319 ft) summit, you're rewarded with outstanding views over Ballater, up towards Lochnagar and right across Deeside and west towards the eastern Cairngorms, a National Scenic Area.

Also on the Invercauld Estate is Keilloch (NO188915) near Braemar. Families in search of a bright open wood to explore could do no better than head for this native Caledonian Scots pine plantation, high above the River Dee, which offers interest, shelter and some stunning views. Peaceful and diverse, the site is home not only to eagles, red squirrels, ptarmigan, deer and a rare mushroom found in only 28 other sites worldwide; it's also a wonderful place to spot Scottish crossbills.

Mar Lodge Estate
Braemar
(NO097899) 29,380 ha (72,600
acres) SSSI, NNR, NSA, NP
National Trust for Scotland

Set in the heart of the
Cairngorms National Park, the
rolling expanse that makes up
Mar Lodge Estate takes in four
out of five of the UK's highest
mountains and one of
Scotland's largest areas of
Scheduled Ancient
Monuments, from post
mediaeval townships to
remnants of early 19th-century
sheep farming.

Home to the rare golden
eagle, this vast estate carries a
unique sense of freedom with
its wild open spaces. You can
drink in stunning scenery,
peacefulness and a rich wildlife
population that includes pine
martens, red deer and red
squirrels. Caledonian pine
forest clothes the landscape and
walkers have a choice of
routes, from low-lying
woodland and riverside walks,
to lofty hilltops and long
distance walks, such as the
Lairig Ghru which leads to
Speyside.

Mar Lodge Estate
© Alan Melrose

Visit in September and you
can enjoy the Braemar
Highland Games, an annual
favourite of the Queen.

Mar Lodge also includes
Glen Quoich (NO119912) an
interesting and beautiful little
wooded glen, full of mystery
and tranquillity. It contains a
number of old twisted pine
trees and is also notable for its
spectacular geological
formation, known as the
Punchbowl. Shaped like a
cauldron, when the river is
high, water swirls around the
Punchbowl, carved out by
tonnes of water pounding away
at it over many years. A
spectacular site, although care is
needed after heavy rainfall.

Craigievar Castle
Alford
(NJ556095) 122 ha (302 acres)
National Trust for Scotland

A secluded hilltop castle in a quiet, scenic parkland, beautiful views and open woodland, all combine to give a 'homely' character to the landscape of this interesting site.

A waymarked walk 'Craigievar Woodland Trail' takes visitors through the woods, marsh and farmland to enjoy the vista across to the castle and hills beyond, while the recently opened Craigievar Hill Trail leads up behind the castle, for a longer walk with views to Lochnager. Take care as there are some steep sections on both trails. A small burn also runs through the property, where improvement work is planned to extend the network of woodland tracks. Visitors may spot bats, roe deer and a host of birds.

Craigevar Castle

© Alan Melrose

Castle Fraser
Dunecht

(NJ725125) 61 ha (150 acres)
National Trust for Scotland

Castle Fraser
© Alan Melrose

A site with real family appeal, the magnificent Castle Fraser combines history, stunning landscapes, rich wildlife, open woodland and a host of activities and features for families, such as 'Woodland Secrets', an area where children can play safely amongst wooded sculptures, a bamboo snake, tepees, a tree house and a stone circle. There is also a grassed amphitheatre called 'Word in the Woods' used for storytelling and poetry.

Red squirrels, bats, roe deer, sparrowhawks and otters make their home among and beneath the beech trees and old sycamores. There's also a pond which is often used by damsel and dragonflies.

© Alan Melrose

Fyvie Castle

Fyvie Castle
Fyvie

(NJ762392) 40 ha (100 acres)

National Trust for Scotland

Stories abound about Fyvie Castle, but the main attraction, apart from the castle itself, is a loch rich in wildlife, plus an interesting old boat house. There is a small mixed woodland, alive with birdsong and explored via well-surfaced, waymarked paths. Wildlife found on site includes red squirrels, wildfowl, otters and bats. There is a choice of short walks around the loch and Fyvie is also part of a longer castle trail, which incorporates 13 other sites through north-east Scotland.

Old Wood of Drum
Drumoak

(NJ792005) 81 ha (200 acres) SSSI

National Trust for Scotland

The Old Wood of Drum is a lovely remnant of an ancient Royal Forest, which forms part of a larger woodland complex around Drum Castle.

The site once produced oaks for the shipbuilding industry, but today it's a peaceful old oak woodland, featuring some lovely old trees where jays, song thrushes and pipistrelle bats number among the thriving wildlife community.

Great for peaceful walks or family outings, the estate has two waymarked woodland trails, with gardens and an adventure playground created within the castle complex.

Also worth a visit is nearby Clune Wood (NO794957), an ancient burial site featuring one of 90 recumbent stone circles unique to Grampian. Three waymarked trails through the wood tell six stories created by local schoolchildren.

Crathes Castle
Banchory
(NO736968) 162 ha (400 acres)
National Trust for Scotland

Once part of the Royal Forest of Drum, Crathes is a big hit with thousands of visitors who flock there each year. It's a delightful mix of a magnificent 16th-century castle, woodland, farmland and lake, all bearing signs of a rich and interesting history.

There's a chance of encountering red squirrels, woodpeckers, buzzards, herons and even otters on a visit to this family favourite, which now features shopping and catering facilities.

There's a choice of woodland trails, via well-maintained paths, from which visitors can enjoy the wealth of historic features – exotic gardens and rocky outcrops, remnants of semi-natural woodland and more recent Scots pine plantation – with the chance to enjoy great views across the Dee Valley.

Crathes Castle
© Alan Melrose

Scolty
Banchory
(NO687947) 1,094 ha (2,703 acres)
Forestry Commission Scotland

Perfect for family walks, this popular conifer-dominated wood is a haven of peace where the views across Deeside are well worth the climb up Scolty Hill.

The paths are in good condition, suitable in places for wheelchairs, and there are lots of trails and routes, including four waymarked routes, to explore. Scolty is actually part of the Blackhall Forest complex which extends to Finzean and Potarch. Another nearby site is Mulloch Wood (NO719913), which encompasses a walk with a series of standing stones called 'Nine Stanes'.

Scolty
© Alan Melrose

Glen Dye
Banchory
(NO645865) 3,240 ha (8,000 acres)
Privately owned

Buzzards and hen harriers fly over the forest and moorland of Glen Dye, a quiet mixed woodland with lovely views, situated on the Victoria Trail.

Great for families, the peaceful surroundings are ideal for wildlife observation and the forest can be explored via a range of forest trails and paths. A climb to the summit of Clachnaben provides the option of a walk down into the Feugh Valley.

Drumtochy Forest (NO698799) accessed via Drumtochy castle is also nearby and well worth a visit.

Leith Hall Woodland
Kennethmont
(NJ542297) 40 ha (100 acres)
National Trust for Scotland

A peaceful slice of the Scottish countryside, Leith Hall includes a charming house, beautiful landscaped gardens, coniferous woodland and open moorland. It offers lovely views of the surrounding hills, particularly from the top of Craig Fall Hill – and, it's believed, is one of only a few places in Scotland to find blunt-leaved bristle moss. The woodland, inhabited by roe deer, wildfowl, various birds, otters and dippers, is served by a number of waymarked trails.

Another nearby site is Clashindarroch Forest (NJ579328) which also includes a range of trails. Three sites on the edges of Clashindarroch, collectively known as Darroch Wids, are part of a large-scale native woodland restoration project which aims to recreate the landscape that existed in these parts centuries ago. Species such as birch, oak, ash, rowan and aspen have been planted with large areas of open space and a newly planted wildflower meadow, that in time will become home to much of the area's local flora and fauna. There are a number of rough walking routes throughout each of the sites.

Leith Hall Woodland
© Alan Melrose

Aberdeen Woods
Aberdeen
(NJ870045) 1,008 ha (2,491 acres)
Forestry Commission Scotland

The Aberdeen Woods is a circle of six relatively new woods that surround the city of Aberdeen, providing a ring of green, wildlife-filled havens for the city's inhabitants.

Each wood has its own character and history, but three of them – Countesswells, Rotten O'Gairn and Foggieton Woods – are linked by paths. They offer an escape to the countryside and the chance to spot red and grey squirrels, roe deer, plus a variety of birds and butterflies. One of the woods, Tyrebagger Forest has a 'Robbers Cave', where 17th-century thieves used to hide out, while Kirkhill Forest has the Tappie Tower, with views out to sea and over the city.

Aberdeen Woods
© Alan Melrose

Haddo
Ellon
(NJ875345) 73 ha (180 acres)
Aberdeenshire Council

Set around one of Scotland's grandest stately homes, this peaceful country park is listed as an outstanding example of the landscape styles of its day.

It's a mix of open water, mature tree-planting and grassland with a huge array of wild flowers and woodland.

A variety of woodland birds, a host of different tree species, fungi and wildflowers, all add to the rich diversity of wildlife

© Alan Melrose

Haddo

at Haddo.

A good place to spend an afternoon with the family, the paths are in excellent condition, and there are a number of walks of varying lengths – all waymarked.

Gight Wood
Ellon

(NJ820392) 36 ha (89 acres) SSSI
Scottish Wildlife Trust

 P

Remote, exciting, and teeming with wildlife, Gight Wood lies on steep slopes overlooking the tightly winding River Ythan. The ruins of Gight Castle, once home to Lord Byron, tower over the wood, which is full of oak, ash, elm, birch and wild cherry, the latter of which brightens the gorge woods with its wonderful spring blossom. A good track leads through the wood (though the going can be muddy) and the bridge at the top is a great place for spotting otter and red squirrel.

121

Aden Country Park
© Alan Melrose

Aden Country Park
Peterhead
(NJ986475) 93 ha (230 acres)
Aberdeenshire Council

Aden Country Park is home to a wealth of wildlife – from roe deer, ducks and waterfowl to a host of woodland birds and osprey – all of which you can enjoy from a bird hide by the small lake on site.

Mixed woodlands including established areas of conifer plantations and other parts, (where the plantations have been replaced by native broadleaf trees and shrubs) a river and lake combine with open, grassy spaces to create a wildlife haven and beautiful surroundings for a family day out.

Miles of surfaced paths provide ample opportunity to explore the park, and a range of shopping and catering facilities are available in the centre of the park. A wheelchair-friendly sensory garden adds another element of interest.

Bennachie
Inverurie
(NJ665225) 2,413 ha (5,963 acres)
Forestry Commission Scotland

Legends and myths abound at Bennachie, adding a fascinating strand to the wealth of other interesting features that make this such a rewarding place to visit.

The site features conifer woodland of varying age and type and broadleaf woods of oak and birch. These are complemented by open moorland, dominated by ling heather and wetter areas where cotton grass, bog asphodel, sundew and butterwort thrive. Roe deer, red squirrel, great spotted woodpecker and various birds of prey also feature among the rich wildlife population of the site, through which a number of burns wend their way.

There's a choice of walks through the area – something to suit all tastes.

Dunnottar Woodland Park
Stonehaven
(NO862844) 34 ha (84 acres)
Forestry Commission Scotland

Just a walk away from a busy town centre, you can immerse yourself in the tranquillity of this picturesque woodland close to Dunnottar Castle. Though finding the site itself can be a little challenging, once you get there the wood is full of wonderful plant and animal life, such as red squirrel, roe deer and dippers, which can be enjoyed via a choice of trails along good clear paths. Glasslaw Burn also runs through the site.

Dunnottar Woodland Park

© Alan Melrose

Denlethen Wood
Laurencekirk
(NO700703) 68 ha (168 acres)
Forestry Commission Scotland

The small conifer wood, an 'oasis' of trees surrounded by arable farmland, is an important habitat for wild creatures, from wood mice, voles and shrews to red squirrel, jays, damselflies and butterflies.

There's a pond in the heart of the site, with open grassy areas around the edges and clearings that have been cut through the wood to show views of the surrounding area.

Moray

Glenlivet Estate
Tomintoul
(NJ170250) 23,470 ha (58,000 acres) NP
The Crown Estate
www.glenlivetestate.co.uk

Vast and scenic, historic and diverse, the highland estate of Glenlivet encompasses forests and farms, rushing rivers and rolling hills and a wealth of family activities – and all in the heart of Scotland's whisky country.

This massive estate, part of the Cairngorms National Park and owned by the Crown Estates, lies between the Ladder and the Cromdale Hills. It encompasses a number of woods with a plethora of well-presented walks to choose from, varying from forest strolls to moorland hikes. This is a stunning opportunity to find solitude and peace within a vast landscape.

Many of the routes offer stunning views across the estate and there's a nature trail with background on the vibrant wildlife, which includes siskins and goldcrests, red squirrels and short-eared owls, buzzards and sparrowhawks.

History has left its mark all over the site, from a battlefield

Glenlivet Estate

© Jamie Cowie

and old military bridge, to an old seminary and castle, all of which make popular destinations for tourists who flock to this area.

Facilities for visitors are excellent and the landscape forms an idyllic base for mountain biking and horse-riding, orienteering and clay pigeon shooting, canoeing, salmon and trout fishing and both downhill and cross-country skiing.

Glenlivet is also a perfect base for touring and many other attractions lie within easy reach, including the beaches and fishing villages of the Moray coast and the castle country of Grampian. The estate also lies on the famous Malt Whisky Trail, with a range of local distilleries close at hand.

Culbin Forest
Forres
(NH981599) 3,000 ha (7,413 acres)
Forestry Commission Scotland

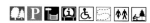

With more than 130 different species of lichen alone to be found within Culbin Forest, it's little wonder this extensive forest is renowned for its biodiversity.

Culbin is the largest continuous plantation in the Moray district and it occupies an imposing position on the vast sand dune area of the ▸▸

Culbin Forest

© Jamie Cowie

coast between Nairn and Findhorn Bay. It offers some wonderful views across the Moray Firth.

One of its most unusual features is the 'Buried Tree', and the forest is often used as an educational base for schools and nature groups, as well as being popular with cyclists and horse-riders, not to mention the families, day-trippers and walkers who make full use of the chance to explore its flat terrain.

The rich wildlife population in the area, which includes roe deer, red squirrel, badgers, seals and pine martens, has been increased thanks to a man-made gravel pit pond, along with a duck and wildlife pond.

Darnaway Forest
Forres
(NH994536) 2,000 ha (5,000 acres)
Privately owned

It's 'adults only' if you're tackling a walk through the woods of the dramatic River Findhorn gorge. This mixed woodland site, part of the Darnaway Castle estate, is popular with anglers but the terrain is too treacherous for the very young and infirm.

However, those who do take on the challenge can enjoy views across the gorge and Darnaway and potentially spot red squirrels, roe deer and, in late summer, peacock and red admiral butterflies.

There are also lots of interesting sites to see nearby, including Randolph's Leap, Brodie Castle (see below) and several distilleries.

Darnaway Forest
© Jamie Cowie

© Jamie Cowie

Brodie Castle

Brodie Castle
Forres
(NH980578) 71 ha (175 acres)
National Trust for Scotland

The picturesque surroundings of Brodie Castle, with its man-made lake, include a formal woodland with a variety of trees.

The wood is perfect for families who can enjoy a walk around the pond, feed the ducks and swans, or take advantage of the bird hide. Opposite the wood is a large open area of lawn and an avenue of lime and copper beech trees.

Altyre Woods
Cannich
(NJ021529) 1,000 ha (2,471 acres)
Privately owned

This large and quiet complex of mixed woodland lies on low, flat terrain that can be explored from a single walk that follows the long-distance route of the Dava Way.

Overgrown in places, the path follows an old railway cutting across farm and forest tracks, crossing tributaries of the River Findhorn as it wends its way through the woods.

© Jamie Cowie

Binn Hill

Binn Hill
Garmouth
(NJ306649) 136 ha (336 acres)
Privately owned

It's just a short walk through the hillside woods to the top of Binn Hill and the chance to drink in beautiful panoramic views right across the Moray Firth to Lossiemouth.

This privately-owned plantation, inhabited by roe deer and red squirrels, is served by many paths and trails but has no waymarked walk. However, the route to the top is well used by local people.

Millbuies Country Park
Elgin
(NJ243570) 65 ha (160 acres)
Moray Council

Impressive mature larch trees stand out among the conifers lining the slopes above the man-made fishery lake of Millbuies Country Park.

It's a tranquil setting, with leisurely lakeside walks and hillside paths leading through to a high path offering views right across the Moray Firth. Wildlife includes wildfowl, amphibians, rabbits, red squirrels and roe deer. And in the spring the rhododendrons and planted azaleas are a colourful delight.

Another nearby site, also managed by Moray Council and the Forestry Commission, is Quarrel Wood (NJ189632). Situated on top of a hill overlooking Elgin, Quarrel is an attractive semi-natural oakwood with pine plantations on the upper slope and includes good facilities, interesting walks and easy accessibility for everybody. It also has a range of information boards highlighting the historical and natural

Millbuies Country Park
© Jamie Cowie

importance of the wood in Moray.

Fachabers & Slorachs Woods

Fochabers
(NJ344589) 351 ha (867 acres)
Forestry Commission Scotland

Fochabers and Slorachs Wood is a popular spot with locals, who enjoy its combination of good walks and interesting landmarks, plus new mountain bike trails.

Local folklore tells the tragic story of a local woman who made her home in the woodland and died below the stone in Slorach's Wood. This, plus numerous tales of bandits using them, adds to the intrigue surrounding the maze of paths that lead through the hillside woods, planted originally by the Duke of Gordon and Richmond.

There's a good variety of waymarked trails, winding walks and lovely views across the Spey Valley; while the popular Speyside Walk also runs near this site.

TAYSIDE & FIFE

© Felicity Martin

Pass of Killiecrankie

Once in Tayside you are deep in 'Big Tree Country', for nowhere else in Scotland will you come upon so many huge, old specimen trees, both native and introduced. The woods around Dunkeld hold several national champions, both in terms of size and longevity.

The meandering Tay, fed from the loch by Fortingall, and the Tummel, which swells the flow south of Pitlochry, offer tree-clad splendour all along their courses – a glorious mixture of the natural and the planted, never more vibrant than in autumn.

In low-lying Fife a different array of woods may be discovered, often associated with large historic houses or on the edges of communities, they offer a greater diversity of broadleaf species than up country and, on the coast, you get the added bonus of the sea birds and seals.

ARCHIE MILES

Map
no.

See map overleaf for wood locations ▶▶

MAP 7 - TAYSIDE & FIFE

Please refer to page 131 for wood names and details of further information.

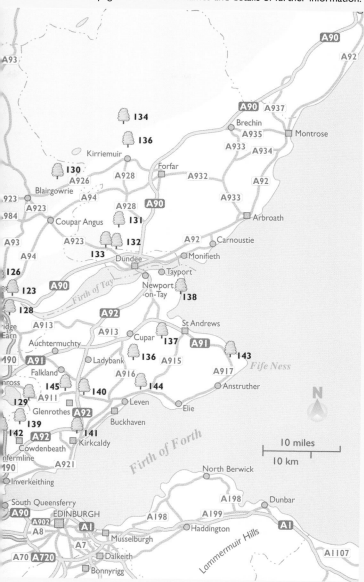

A90
A92
A93
A93

134
136

Brechin
A90 A937
A935
Montrose
A933 A934
Kirriemuir
Forfar
130
A926
A928
A932
A92
Blairgowrie
A94
A933
923
A923
A928 A90
131
984
Coupar Angus
Arbroath
A93
A923
132
A92 Carnoustie
A94
133
Dundee
Monifieth
126
Tayport
123
Firth of Tay
Newport
-on-Tay
138
128
A90
A92
idge
A913
St Andrews
Earn
A913
Cupar 137
190 A91
Auchtermuchty
136 A915
A91
143
Fife Ness
nross
Ladybank
A916
144
A917
145
Falkland
140
A917
Anstruther
nross
A911
129
Leven
Elie
Glenrothes A92
139
Buckhaven
142 A92
141
Firth of Forth
Cowdenbeath
Kirkcaldy
nfermline
A921
North Berwick
190
Inverkeithing
A198
Dunbar
South Queensferry
A198
A199
A90
EDINBURGH
A902
A8
A1
A7
Haddington
Musselburgh
A70 A720
Dalkeith
Lammermuir Hills
A1107
Bonnyrigg

10 miles
10 km

The above map is a guide only. Please contact relevant organisations for more detailed location information.

Perth & Kinross

The Hermitage
Dunkeld
(NO013423) 13 ha (32 acres)
NSA
The National Trust for Scotland

An impressive woodland set dramatically on the north bank of the River Braan, the Hermitage is bedecked with a delightful mixture of waterfalls, rocks, tall imposing trees and intriguing man-made features, including Ossian's Hall.

A waymarked trail runs

through the wood, and both the Braan and Inver walks run through it. In spring the site is adorned with snowdrops and bluebells, and there's always the possibility of spotting red squirrels.

The site shares its entrance with another wood, the Craigvinean Forest (NO007419), an extensive forest owned by Forestry Commission Scotland, which covers the hillside on the west side of the Tay. It was created in the 18th century by larch seed brought from the Alps.

A number of woods and woodland walks owned by Atholl Estates also run near the Hermitage:

Craig a 'Barns is the name given to the forested crags north of Dunkeld, which the Duke of Atholl planted by firing seeds from a canon. It's the start of a large wooded and open area that runs north for miles and has a good network of old estate tracks (some used on carriage drives by Queen Victoria when she visited).

The Hermitage
© Felicity Martin

The Atholl Woods Walk circuits the crags, passing Mill Dam (a loch), and has some lovely views over the Tay Valley. You might see fallow deer, roe deer, red squirrels and in summer, osprey and buzzards.

The Dunkeld Riverside Walk (NO025426) is another attractive route which follows the River Tay and then the River Braan. There is a lovely woodland and some fine specimen trees on route and in autumn, beautiful leaf colours are reflected in the river.

Craig Wood (NO035426) east of Dunkeld, is also worth a visit, being famed for its bluebell displays in spring.

Pass of Killiecrankie
Pitlochry

(NN916627) 22 ha (55 acres)
SSSI, NSA
The National Trust for Scotland

Pass of Killiecrankie
© Felicity Martin

For centuries the Pass of Killiecrankie has been a major link between the highlands and lowlands of Scotland and also marks the site of a historic Jacobite battle. This was the route taken by advancing lowland forces ahead of the Battle of Killiecrankie in 1689.

The steep-sided hillsides are covered in a mature mixed woodland which fill this dramatic, narrow gorge and offers fantastic views that are particularly vibrant in spring and autumn. Red squirrels, small woodland birds, ducks ▶▶

and red-breasted merganser frequent the area. A popular destination for travellers and locals, many stop at the Garry Bridge car park to enjoy the dramatic view of Carn Liath.

The Linn of Tummel (NN910600) can also be accessed from Garry Bridge. This feature used to be called the Falls of Tummel; however, the falls were reduced in height after the creation of Loch Faskally (as part of a 1950 hydro-electric scheme) and so were renamed. Walkers can continue from here up to Coronation Bridge, a suspension bridge opened on the coronation day of King George V in 1911.

Craigower Hill (NN937593) can be found near the north end of Pitlochry. Also owned by the National Trust for Scotland, it can be accessed from the car park at Balnacraig Farm and has a superb summit looking west over Loch Tummel and Loch Rannoch towards the Glencoe Hills. It's heathery top is great for Scotch argus butterflies and the route up and over the hill is part of the Pitlochry Walks Network.

Faskally Forest
Pitlochry
(NN922592) 364 ha (900 acres)
Forestry Commission Scotland

Faskally Forest
© Felicity Martin

Tranquil, scenic and welcoming to visitors of all abilities, Faskally Forest is an attractive wood with many water features and a variety of trees.

Many of the trees, which include Scots pine and Douglas fir, date back 200 years and provide shelter for red squirrels, while herons and waterfowl thrive on Loch Faskally.

Black Spout (NN950575) is a nearby oakwood, managed by Perth & Kinross Council. It lies between two burns – one of which runs through a gorge and over the Black Spout waterfall. The waymarked Edradour Walk, which also forms part of the Pitlochry

Walks network, runs through the site linking the Edradour Distillery (Scotland's smallest) with Blair Athol Distillery on the other side of the wood.

Allean Forest
Pitlochry
(NN857600) 863 ha (2,133 acres)
Forestry Commission Scotland

Many parts of this steep hillside conifer plantation above Loch Tummel boast tall, mature trees dating back more than a century, confirming the site's

credentials as part of 'Perthshire Big Tree Country'.

The forest features larch, Scots pine and Sitka spruce, enjoyed from a good network of paths. Several small burns run down the hillside, which also has a number of archaeological sites.

The Queen's View, Allean Forest

© Felicity Martin

© Felicity Martin

Black Wood of Rannoch

Black Wood of Rannoch
Kinloch Rannoch

(NN617570) 631 ha (1,559 acres)
SSSI

Forestry Commission Scotland

A remnant of an ancient Caledonian forest and now part of the Tay Forest Park, this eastern part of Rannoch Forest now contains a mix of more modern conifer plantations and an area of mature oakwood and native broadleaves along the Allt na Bogair, a burn with steep riverbanks.

The site contains a number of 'granny pines' of great age and there are two pleasant walks, both waymarked from nearby Kinloch Rannoch. One runs along the riverside and the other passes the Allt Mor waterfall, then goes past Loch Rannoch, returning along the river past a picnic site and a small hydro dam.

Drummond Hill
Aberfeldy

(NN770460) 1,026 ha (2,535 acres)
Forestry Commission Scotland

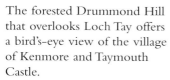

The forested Drummond Hill that overlooks Loch Tay offers a bird's-eye view of the village of Kenmore and Taymouth Castle.

The wood is said to be Scotland's first managed forest – it was planted in the 17th century – and has a number of mature trees, supporting red squirrels, roe deer, Scottish crossbills and goldcrests. There are two waymarked paths and cycle trails.

It is worth a look at the village of Kenmore itself while visiting this site. A model village, it contains whitewashed buildings with black timbers and the Kenmore Hotel – Scotland's oldest inn – established in 1572. Robert Burns stayed there in 1782 and wrote a poem in pencil above the fireplace, where it can still be seen protected by a sheet of glass.

While in the area, it is also worth visiting the Falls of Acharn, Taymouth Castle and the Fortingall Yew. The latter, situated at Fortingall village churchyard at the north side of Drummond Hill, dates between 3,000–9,000 years old and is believed to be the oldest living organism in Europe.

Drummond Hill
© Felicity Martin

Glen Lednock Circuit
Comrie
(NN777223) 100 ha (247 acres)
SSSI, NSA
Forestry Commission Scotland

Part of a stunning landscape and Perth and Kinross' largest area of native oak woodland, this oft-visited wooded valley boasts a rich variety of mossy oaks and mature beeches and a wealth of plants and animals, including dippers, buzzards and bluebells.

Among the star attractions of this beautiful site are the spectacular views of Dell's Cauldron, a waterfall which plunges dramatically into a pothole. It is also worth visiting Comrie Village while in the area, a conservation village protected for its period architecture.

Glen Lednock Circuit

© Felicity Martin

Kinnoull Hill Woodland Park
Perth
(NO145236) 300 ha (741 acres)
SSSI
Forestry Commission Scotland and Perth & Kinross Council

A Perthshire Big Tree Country site, for well over a decade the extensive woodland park of Kinnoull Hill has been a popular haven for the people of Perth.

The River Tay winds past, beneath the line of cliffs that border Kinnoull Hill, the latter an impressive landscape feature topped by a cliff-edge folly.

Walking, wildlife studies, picnicking, riding and cycling are all popular activities across the site, a combination of the mainly broadleaved Kinnoull Hill and Barnhill and the conifer-dominated Corsiehill and Deuchny Wood, along with neighbouring Binn Hill.

Red squirrels and a range of woodland plants and birds make this a rich wildlife habitat and there's a chance to discover history with the remains of an Iron Age hill fort in Deuchny Wood.

There are fantastic views from within the attractive mature woodland and its popularity is evident from the maze of paths that have been trodden by its many visitors. A new 5 km (3 mile) network of paths offers easy access to a large part of the hill and includes a short loop suitable for wheelchairs.

Kinnoull Hill Woodland Park
© Felicity Martin

Knock of Crieff
Crieff
(NN865226) 30 ha (74 acres)
**Perth & Kinross Council and
various private owners**

Home to the red squirrel, the
Knock of Crieff is a long hill
with panoramic views of fertile
lowland plains and the
beautiful highland mountains.

The woodland is a mixture of
conifer plantation and
deciduous trees. Families can
enjoy the short walk to the
viewpoint and there are lots of
other trails too, as the wood is
on the Crieff Walks network.
This includes Lady Mary's
Walk, a popular and accessible
beauty spot, which runs beside
the River Earn under mature
beeches, Scots pine, sweet
chestnut and larch.

Birks of Aberfeldy
Aberfeldy
(NN855486) 42 ha (104 acres)
Perth & Kinross Council

Considered an area of high
conservation value, the Birks of
Aberfeldy – the name penned
by Robert Burns – is a
wooded site lying on the south
side of a glacial valley with a
cascading burn. A wide variety
of birds and plants, some of
them rare, can be found on the
site, which can be explored via
a network of well-maintained
paths and boardwalks.

Also worth a visit is nearby

Birks of Aberfeldy
© Felicity Martin

Weem Forest (NN838497). This Forestry Commission Scotland site is just across the Wade Bridge from Aberfeldy in Weem, adjacent to Castle Menzies. It forms a particularly attractive and colourful backdrop to the castle in autumn.

A short, steep and rough waymarked trail circuits this predominantly broadleaved wood, which grows among the crags of Weem Rock. There are several legends linked with the caves found here and a number of wood carvings around the wood reflect these myths, such as the story of Christian missionary St Cuthbert who lived as a hermit in one of them.

Scone Palace
Scone
(NO115265) 40 ha (100 acres)
Privately owned
www.scone-palace.co.uk

The grounds of this historic palace mix parkland and woodland around a Gothic-Georgian mansion at the heart of Scotland's former capital.

Originally laid out 200 years ago, the grounds offer some beautiful prospects. Suited for visitors of all ages and abilities, this lovely mixed setting has a variety of interesting features, including a maze, some heritage trees and a stunning pinetum.

The pinetum contains avenues consisting of the same species, including some of Scotland's finest giant redwoods, noble firs and ▶▶

Scone Palace
© Felicity Martin

143

monkey puzzles. Look out for the King James VI sycamore, planted by the monarch on his only return visit to Scotland after the Union of the Crowns.

The paths around the palace are very good, but become more uneven as you explore deeper into the woods. A nature walk has also been created around the wooded den of Catmoor Burn. The western edge of the grounds is marked by the fast-flowing River Tay and Scone Palace itself is well worth a look.

Nearby Scone Palace, you'll find Muirward Wood (NO140280) which contains a massive Scots pine known as the 'King of the Forest' – with the largest girth recorded for this species in the UK. Also worth a visit is nearby North Wood (NO160400) near Meikleour. Popular with locals, it contains an important Scheduled Ancient Monument – the Cleaven Dyke, which dates back to Neolithic times. Meikleour also contains the Meikleour Beech Hedge. Planted in 1745, it is recorded in the Guinness Book of Records as the highest hedge in the world.

Glen Quey
Dollar
(NN988020) 383 ha (946 acres)
Woodland Trust Scotland

You need to be fit to reach the summit of Innerdownie in the Ochills, which is 611 metres (2,005 ft) above sea level, but it's worth it for the spectacular panoramic views. On a clear day, you can see far out into the Firth of Forth and if you look north mountains, such as Ben Vorlich and Schiehallion, are clearly visible. Below this, you can find the newly established native woodland at Glen Quey.

Overlooking Glen Devon village and having a small frontage to the Devon River, Glen Quey is one of three sites in the Ochil Hills, the other two being Glen Sherup and Geordie's Wood, on which the Woodland Trust Scotland is creating native woods.

Glen Quey Wood is the result of planting over half a million native trees. The woodland has been carefully designed so that the rolling ridges of Innerdownie are still left clear of trees. It's now a place where less-common species, such as the pearl-bordered fritillaries, spotted flycatchers, song thrushes, redstarts and wood warblers can thrive. Birds of prey, such as short-eared owls, sparrowhawks and kestrels, are now a far more common sight, thanks to the perch poles placed to attract them.

A popular walk is to follow

Glen Quey
© WTPL/Niall Benvie

the old drove road through Glen Quey that runs between Castle Campbell in Dollar Glen and Glen Devon.

Moncreiffe Hill Wood
Bridge of Earn
(NO138197) 130 ha (333 acres)
Woodland Trust Scotland

As its name suggests, magnificent Moncreiffe Hill Wood occupies a prominent position on a hill boasting panoramic views over Perth, the Tay, Strathearn, Fife and the Lomond hills.

Moncreiffe Hill is a beautiful mix of broadleaves and conifers, spectacular in its autumn colours and with some impressive veteran Douglas firs.

It's home to red squirrels, green and great spotted woodpeckers,

buzzards, sparrowhawks and jays, plus a varied range of ground flora, including wild strawberry, wood sage and lady's smock. There are some locally rare species too, such as scarlet pimpernel, crow garlic, the deep pink jewel-like common centaury, orange hawkweed and the delicate blue forget-me-nots found on the crags at the top of the hill. Listen for the scuttle of red squirrels in the larch trees and look out for buzzards soaring above you. Watch out also for the evergreen stinking hellebore, the name speaks for itself!

With a 14 km (8.6 mile) network of surfaced paths, Moncreiffe Hill offers ▸▸

excellent walks suitable for everyone. Visitors can chose from one of three waymarked trails, including an ambling stroll around the almost-level track along the base of the hill, or a more vigorous circuit up through the crags to the plateau and hill fort at its highest point. Stop to admire one of the spectacular viewpoints overlooking the Perthshire landscape along the way. The ground is steep in places so care should be taken.

Moncreiffe Hill Wood
© WTPL/Jane Button

Portmoak Moss
Scotlandwell
(NO183015) 43 ha (106 acres)
Woodland Trust Scotland

One of central Scotland's few remaining areas of raised peat bog, Portmoak Moss is an open mosaic of sphagnum moss, heather and grasses, surrounded by woodland. It contains up to eight different species of sphagnum moss and 22 different species of breeding birds, such as great spotted woodpeckers, long-eared owls

and goldcrest. While roe deer, red squirrels and the most recent inhabitants – pipistrelle bats (using special boxes put up by the local support group) also frequent the site.

In the Middle Ages, Portmoak was part of a much larger uncultivated bog that provided peat, turf and pasture for local people and this practice continued right up until the 20th century. The site is now being restored by the Woodland Trust Scotland after many years of conifer planting.

A 4.8 km (3 mile) circular walk called the Michael Bruce

Trail (after a local poet) links Portmoak Moss with another Woodland Trust Scotland site nearby. A contrasting site Kilmagad (NO185020) is a mix of broadleaved woodland and open ground, which lies on the steep slopes of the Lomond Hills and has outstanding long-distance views across Loch Leven and beyond.

Potmoak Moss
© Andy Fairbairn

Den of Alyth
Alyth
(NO236486) 22 ha (54 acres) SSSI
Perth & Kinross Council

The high cliffs and deep valley of the Den of Alyth, with Alyth Burn running through its heart, have proved a tranquil haven for woodland wildlife for thousands of years. As a result, this rich and vibrant site has an abundance of wildlife and plant species – little wonder it's been designated as a Site of Special Scientific Interest.

However, the once-popular practice of planting ▸▸

Den of Alyth
© Felicity Martin

non-native trees has changed the character of the site. Its western bank, unruly and natural, boasts a mix of native broadleaved trees and shrubs, with a rich under-storey. On the eastern bank, sections are dominated by mature beech.

Facilities at the site include a playpark and picnic area and a network of paths, which can get narrow and muddy. However, there is also a fully accessible path circuit.

Angus

Balkello Wood
Auchterhouse, Angus
(NO365387) 114 ha (281 acres)
Privately owned

There are stunning views from the top of Balkello Wood, a young site on the slopes of the Sidlaw Hills that's already rich in plant, insect and bird species. There are more than 130 species of flowering plants and 100 types of beetle in this wood.

The mown rides provide a good network of paths through the wood, which ranges from broadleaves on the lower areas to Scots pine on the upper ones. The quarry near the summit, containing 400,000,000-year-old rocks and fossils, is a regionally important geological and geomorphologic site.

Templeton Woods
Dundee
(NO360341) 58 ha (144 acres)
Dundee City Council

Templeton Woods link with Camperdown Park and Clatto Reservoir and together they provide a great habitat for wildlife and excellent facilities for visitors, including an art trail, pond, adventure playpark, trampoline, boats, golf course, water sports, fishing, a wildlife and visitor centre with refreshments. The woodland is

148

mixed and populated by red squirrels, roe deer, rabbits, tawny owls and jays. There's a network of paths and trails suitable for pedestrians, horse-riders and mountain bikers.

Templeton Woods
© Jill Aitken

Backmuir Wood
Muirhead
(NO341339) 50 ha (122 acres)
Woodland Trust Scotland

Rich and varied, Backmuir Wood is a popular site with a diverse mix of native broadleaved cover, interspersed with stands of planted trees and criss-crossed by several ditches.

There is a good network of paths and a Millennium feature designed by the local community group who help to manage the wood.

A huge beech tree stands in the middle, while other tree species found there include oak, alder, birch, sycamore, Scots pine and Norway spruce. A wide variety of birds, including kestrels and buzzards use the wood, alongside red squirrels, and a variety of insects and other wildlife.

Backmuir Wood
© Jill Aitken

Tulloch Hill
Kirriemuir
(NO372607) 90 ha (222 acres)
Privately owned
www.airlieestates.com

There is a good choice of walks through the peaceful Scots pine-dominated woodland which clothes Tulloch Hill, part of the Airlie Estates.

Visitors who tackle the steep track along a waymarked route up the final stretch of this tranquil wood, to reach Airlie Monument at the summit, can enjoy some fantastic views to Glen Prosen, Glen Clova and beyond.

Tulloch Hill
© Jill Aitken

Caddam Wood
Kirriemuir
(NO381558) 40 ha (100 acres)
Privately owned by Kinnordy Estates

The unusual mix of mature Scots pine with an under-storey of beech lends an unusual character to this tranquil site on the edge of Kirriemuir.

There's a circular walk around the perimeter of the wood, though the more interesting routes lie within, where roe deer make their home. A Roman road runs diagonally through the wood, though signs are not immediately obvious.

Caddam Wood

© Jill Aitken

Fife

Craighall Den
Ceres
(NO399108) 15 ha (37 acres) SSSI

Fife Council and various private owners

Craighall Den is a fabulous woodland and one of the largest and best remaining examples of semi-natural woodland in north-east Fife. About two fifths of the woodland is classified as ancient woodland and another third is long-established woodland, making this a sizeable part of east Fife's entire ancient and long-established woodland resource.

Stunning views, a burn, industrial archaeology and an impressive range of native flora and fauna add to the rich layers of interesting features in this wood, which really does offer 'something for everyone'.

The woodland mix incorporates ash, oak, and elm with locally abundant exotics. An understorey of hazel coppice, elder and hawthorn also has the occasional gooseberry and bird cherry. Bluebells, dog's mercury and greater woodrush feature among a diverse ground flora that guarantees colour all year round.

A well-maintained path runs through the den, before climbing to the site of a former mansion house, which dates back to the 12th or 13th century. There is evidence of various clamp kiln sites, old limestone quarry areas and a sluice over the burn. The best-preserved lime kiln dates back to 1814.

It's particularly worth looking out for the circle of coppiced beech trees near the lime kiln, which bear evidence of the limestone workings.

Craighall Den
© Andrea Partridge

© Duncan Kervell

Bishop's Wood

Bishop's Wood at Magus Muir

Strathkinness, St Andrews

(NO458152) 12 ha (30 acres)

Fife Council

Named after the rather dark history of the murder of Archbishop Sharp of St Andrews in the 16th century, this small, pretty broadleaved wood is a mix of birch, willow and some larger beech and oak trees. Boasting lovely views, it has a good range of facilities and a well-managed path network that suits young and old alike. Look out for a group of yew trees around Archbishop Sharp's memorial cairn.

153

Tentsmuir Forest
Leuchars, Tayport & St Andrews
(NO498242) 1,457 ha (3,200 acres)
SSSI
Forestry Commission Scotland

You can cycle, walk, picnic – and even sledge in winter – or simply enjoy the wonderful sea views that delight visitors to this vast pine plantation, adjacent to the award-winning Kinshaldy beach.

Corsican pine dominates this commercial forest, which has a myriad of potential walks and a strong population of red squirrels to try and spot, plus Scotland's only indigenous bird, the Scottish crossbill.

Lochore Meadows Country Park
Lochgelly
(NT165960) 565 ha (1,400 acres)
Fife Council

Lochore Meadows is a country park in the heart of Lomond Hills. The gently rolling grassland, woodland and loch, provides a major centre for outdoor and environmental education.

The site also includes Harran Hill Wood. This ancient woodland is the only mature wood among a clutch of younger sites. Served by an excellent circular walk leading to the top of the hill, it commands good views over southern Fife and is known as one of the regions 'best bluebell woods' – while also being good for dog's mercury and tawny owls.

Balbirnie Park
Markinch
(NO292019) 168 ha (416 acres)
Fife Council

The woodland walks through this extremely beautiful mixed deciduous woodland are enjoyable, whatever time of year. Once part of the historic Balfour's Estate, Balbirnie Park features more than 60 species of exotic trees, which make it a striking year–round attraction.

The woods can be explored from a varied mix of paths, with some suitable for wheelchairs and pushchairs, although those that lead to the higher viewpoints tend to be steeper, but provide fine views across Fife. The site also includes a craft centre, making it a popular spot for visitors.

At the northern end of the park is a stone circle dating from 2,000 BC, making it the oldest feature of this site. It was once significant as a ritual centre and burial place.

Balbirnie Park

© Andrea Partridge

Dunnikier
Kirkcaldy
(NT283942) 64 ha (158 acres)
Fife Council

The combination of an open parkland setting, mature woodland and some unusual tree varieties make this historic site perfect for a family day out.

The woodland is part of a Historic Designed Landscape around Dunnikier House (now a hotel), much of which survives 200 years on. This impressive site has a good network of paths and trails for exploring the ancient woodland, exotic and unusual trees and its new plantations.

Dunnikier
© Andrea Partridge

Blairadam Forest
Kelty
(NT129945) 1,000 ha (2,471 acres)
Forestry Commission Scotland

Blairadam Forest is a peaceful woodland, inhabited by red squirrels and common lizards, dotted with burns and forest tracks and paths.

The area has a mining heritage going back to the 13th century and there are three waymarked heritage trails and a cycle route through the site, which is mainly conifer plantation with areas of beech, birch and oak.

Cambo Wood
Kingsbarns
(NO599106) 38 ha (93 acres)
Privately owned
www.camboestate.com

Although well worth a visit at any time of the year, February or early March is the best time to visit Cambo Wood, because it's the perfect time to see its outstanding array of snowdrops.

But, there are more than snowdrops – snowflakes and aconites provide a dense woodland carpet that can be enjoyed from the good network of paths that loop through the woodland and a well-signed trail. The ease of access to the coastal paths also makes it ideal for combining a visit to the delightful beach nearby.

The site straddles the Cambo Burn and is part of the renowned Cambo Estate, in what has been described as one of Scotland's most unspoiled areas. Home to the Erskine family since 1688, Cambo House itself was built in 1881 and lies at the heart of the 4,856 hectares (12,000 acre) estate. During spring, special events are often held in the house and there is also a walled garden on the estate. Although the latter has a small entry fee for adults, it's free for children.

Cambo Wood

© Peter Erskine

Keil's Den
Lundin Links
(NO414039) 19 ha (47 acres)
Woodland Trust Scotland

A rich mixture of woodland flowers bear testament to the ancient origins of this gorge woodland – among them a blanket of bluebells, woodrush, dog's mercury, broadbuckler fern and the pungent wild garlic.

This long and narrow wooded glen is intimate and attractive and yet lends an extensive welcome to visitors in the shape of almost 4 km (2.5 miles) of paths providing walking routes of varying lengths.

The boundary path that runs around the rim of the gorge takes visitors through a varied mosaic of woodland featuring most of Scotland's natives, such as ash, birch, rowan, cherry, alder, hazel and Scots pine. A scattering of massive beech trees, planted in a bygone century, are now in elegant decline and increasingly form homes for fungi and a range of insect life.

A surfaced multi-use path, built by a team from the Robert Gough centre, leads from the parking area to a rest area by the Keil Burn.

Keil's Den
© WTPL/Ian Morton

© Niall Benvie

Formonthills
Glenrothes
(NO258035) 120 ha (296 acres)
Woodland Trust Scotland

There is an open feel to this young community woodland, a mix of native broadleaves, Scots pine and shrubs, complemented by belts of mature woodland, wetland areas and glassy glades.

It was created in the mid-1990s with the help of many local people and lies mostly on former farmland – evidence of which is found in the network of ditches and the old drystone dykes. Today, these provide a refuge for wildlife and a link with the past.

Wild flowers, scattered soon after the trees were planted, like primrose, red campion, St John's wort and meadowsweet, provide a blanket of colour for visitors in spring and summer, as well as nectar for bumblebees, butterflies and other insects.

More than 11 km (6.8 miles) of paths provide lots of interesting routes, both soft and surfaced, through the site's level and gently sloping terrain. Some of these lead visitors up to the top of Rhind Hill, where on a clear day there are stunning panoramic views to the south over the Firth of Forth.

More mature woodlands hug the boundary of Glenrothes and paths link into the adjacent Coul Den nature reserve, managed by Fife Council.

HIGHLANDS AND NORTHERN ISLES

© Mike Carter

Glen Affric

The Highlands don't immediately bring woodland to mind, for it is an area largely dominated by treeless mountains and bogs, regarded by many as Europe's last true wilderness. However, the region does contain the western fragments of a Caledonian pine forest, the perfect setting for red deer, golden eagles and those scampering red squirrels. Sites such as Rothiemurchus and Glen Affric offer the very best of the Scots pine forest experience, where it feels as if the trees must have held sway with their understorey of rowan, birch and juniper forever. Not always so. These forests have been cut and replanted or naturally regenerated for many hundreds of years.

The mountains are high and devoid of trees, and it is only around river or loch that any kind of tree cover persists. However, towards the coast there are some wonderful tracts of ancient oak wood, rich in mosses and lichens and offering dreamy sea views out to the Western Isles, which boast their own rugged woods at the limit.

ARCHIE MILES

Map
no.

See map overleaf for wood locations ▸▸

MAP 8 - HIGHLANDS AND NORTHERN ISLES

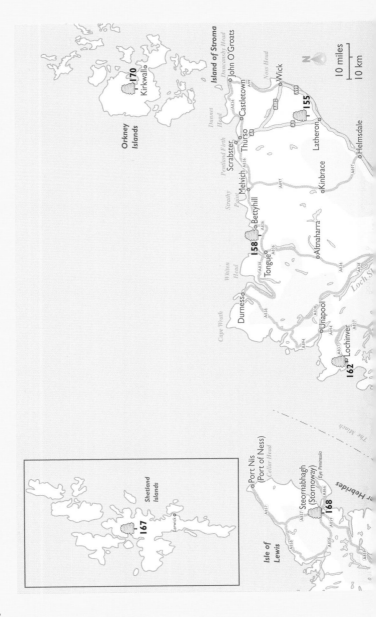

Orkney Islands

170 Kirkwall

Island of Stroma

John O'Groats

Duncansby Head

Ness Head

Wick

155

Castletown

Thurso

Scrabster

Dunnet Head

Pentland Firth

Latheron

Helmsdale

Kinbrace

Melvich

Bettyhill

Strathy

158

Tongue

Altnaharra

Whiten Head

Cape Wrath

Durness

Ullapool

Lochinver

162

Loch S

Port Nis (Port of Ness)

Cellar Head

Seeornabhagh (Stornoway)

168

Eye Peninsula

Isle of Lewis

r Hebrides

The Minch

Shetland Islands

167

Lerwick

N

10 miles
10 km

Please refer to page 161 for wood names and details of further information.

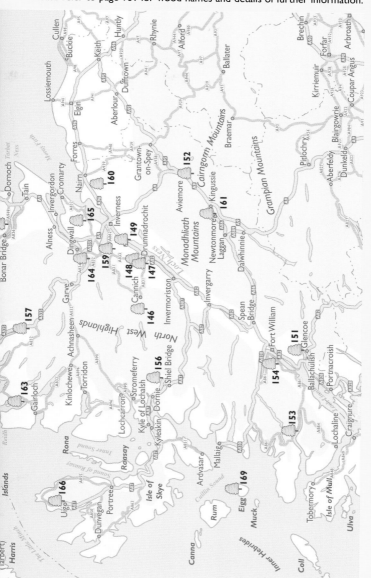

The above map is a guide only. Please contact relevant organisations for more detailed location information.

163

Highlands

Glen Affric
Cannich
(NH284284) 10,000 ha
(24,710 acres) NNR, NSA,
Forestry Commission Scotland

Glen Affric, described by many as 'the most beautiful glen in Scotland', contains one of the country's largest remnants of ancient Caledonian pinewood.

There's little wonder the glen has been designated a Caledonian Forest Reserve, a National Scenic Area and most recently, a National Nature Reserve, with scenery that takes your breath away and some amazing autumn colours.

The mixture of dark green pines, shades of yellow and gold from the birch and the bronze of bracken ensure spectacular displays throughout the glen.

As well as the forest, this vast rural idyll encompasses lochs, moorland and mountains, and

Glen Affric

© Mike Carter

the whole area is a haven for wildlife, including red deer, golden eagle, badger and otter, and even the odd pine marten.

There are several car parks and the site is well served with visitor facilities. The forest roads are ideal for cycling and horse-riding and a variety of long-distance hill walking routes can be accessed from here. There is also a choice of waymarked walks of various lengths – and of course, those majestic views.

Nearby you'll also find the RSPB's Corrimony Nature Reserve (NH348285) a

peaceful mix of conifer plantation, native woodland and moorland, set on gently sloping hills with views across Glen Urquhart.

The site is being developed as a mixed woodland for the benefit of the rapidly declining black grouse. As in Glen Affric non-native tree species are being removed and replaced with birch, rowan, willow, juniper and Scots pine.

Access to the reserve is by foot, and there is waymarked path to Loch Comhnard, which is an 8 km (5 mile) round trip.

Balmacaan Wood
Drumnadrochit
(NH499289) 34 ha (97 acres)
Woodland Trust Scotland

Woodland Trust Scotland's first acquisition, Balmacaan Wood once formed part of an ancient woodland around Loch Ness.

Although the wood is still dominated by oak, during the 20th century the Balmacaan Estate planted many more types of native trees used in local industry, including ash, elm,

chestnut, hazel and alder, and introduced some exotic trees, such as giant redwood or Wellingtonia, Douglas fir, Lawson cypress and rhododendron. A grand fir, one of the largest trees of its type in Scotland, still stands in the wood measuring a mighty 45 metres (150 ft) in height and 8 metres (25 ft) in girth.

The site is rich in wildlife, including mammals like red squirrel and pine martens, birds, such as great spotted woodpeckers, red starts, crossbills and tawny owls, plus vibrant ▸▸

Balmacaan Wood
© Andy Fairbairn

spring-blooming flora, including bluebells and dog's mercury, which are indicative of ancient woodland.

A compact site, it's served by a good network of footpaths, tracks and waymarked walks, and features the cliff-top remains of an Iron Age fort, which is popular with visitors. Look out also for a well-preserved Victorian ice house – one of the few remaining estate buildings left.

You might also like to walk up to Craig Monie – a rocky crag which stands at the north summit of the wood. Visible for miles around, it is named after a Viking prince, Monie, who landed at Argyll with his men, but was chased north by locals and finally reached this rocky crag. A battle was fought and Monie was killed. During the 20th century, Craig Monie was a popular destination for visitors staying at Balmacaan Estate and is still a local landmark.

Urquhart Bay Wood
Drumnadrochit

(NH519297) 24 ha (59 acres)
SSSI, SAC

Woodland Trust Scotland

One of Scotland's best remaining swamp alderwoods and a very rare floodplain forest for the area, Urquhart Bay is a rich mix of broadleaves, including alder, ash, bird cherry, willow, oak and the occasional wych-elm. Fast-flowing rivers run through the wood contributing to its alluvial nature, and it's dotted with old river beds and ponds.

Like Balmacaan, historic Urquhart Bay is part of the large stretch of ancient woodland around Loch Ness – hence it's also a good place to look out for the well-known monster. It's easy to reach and explore, thanks to a well-surfaced path, although in winter this can be more

© WTPL/Roger Warhurst

Urquhart Bay Wood

difficult when the rivers are in full flow.

Rich moss and mature lichen communities thrive in the damp atmosphere and it's teeming with other wildlife too. The site sustains many rare species – including buzzards, bats, otters and many important invertebrate species, including a notable collection of craneflies and hoverflies.

Abriachan Wood
Drumnadrochit
(NH574357) 164 ha (405 acres)
Woodland Trust Scotland

Visitors flock to Abriachan Wood, an ancient semi-natural woodland site that covers a long stretch of the steeply sloping northern shores of Loch Ness.

History has it that the wood provided hidden routes for smugglers to move illicit goods to and from the loch. Today, Abriachan (which means 'mouth of the steep burn') has panoramic views and a surprising array of different woodland types. The wood mainly consists of birch, with areas of oak, alder, aspen, ▸▸

167

wych-elm, juniper and holly. Extensive hazel woodland rich in lichens dominate the lower slopes close to the loch, while a small area of oak nestles in the southwest corner.

It is an important wildlife habitat, with otters, red squirrels, the wildcat, pine martens, and many bat species all present. Merlin and peregrine falcon are also found nesting here. The acid soil is punctuated by unexpected pockets of richer ground, giving rise to bluebells and a variety of other flowers, including enchanter's nightshade, golden rod and sanicle.

Woodland Trust Scotland is encouraging the regeneration of native trees on site, together with some oak, ash and aspen planting, and the removal of non-native planted conifers. This should open up spectacular views of Loch Ness and create glades to encourage other species, such as butterflies like the Scotch argus and speckled wood.

The network of old tracks and rights of way have also been extended to create circular walks, which are popular with locals and visitors alike. Trails at the top of the wood link with a wide network of walks in the woods managed by Abriachan Forest Trust. The Funeral Trail runs through this wood. Little is known about this intriguing right of way, but research is currently being done to find out more.

Abriachan Wood
© WTPL/Roger Warhurst

Ledmore and Migdale
Spinningdale, Bonar Bridge
(NH661904) 710 ha (1,756 acres)
SSSI, NSA, SAC
Woodland Trust Scotland

Priceless for its remarkable variety of wildlife habitats and the hugely varied flora and fauna, Ledmore and Migdale is set in a big sweeping landscape of mountains, moors and glens. It's located on the north shore of Dornoch Firth, within the Dornoch Firth National Scenic Area and surrounds the attractive Spinningdale Loch.

Covering three distinct hills and steep-sided valleys, it offers spectacular views of the West Sutherland mountains. The woods are mixture of Scots pine, oak, birch, alder and willow, with some other conifers. Notably, it contains a particularly large colony of juniper and also has areas of heather moorland, valley bog, open water, reedbeds and rocky crags. One of these is Migdale Rock, which rises 300 metres (985 ft) above sea level at its summit.

Widely recognised as extremely high value for wildlife and people, it contains no fewer than three separate Sites of Special Scientific Interest, including the evocatively named 'Spinningdale Bog' – the only valley bog in East Sutherland.

Alongside these, it also has a treasure trove of archaeological features, from prehistoric chambered cairns to post-medieval townships.

The flora is also extremely rich, with bogbean, common reed, heather and blaeberry just a few examples, and the fauna equally so: black grouse, wood willow warblers, redstarts, tawny owls, buzzards, ospreys, and the endangered Scottish crossbill, all inhabit this site. Red and roe deer, pine martens, red squirrels, otters and even the elusive wild cat – have also been seen.

Visitors can choose from a series of graded walks, one of which leads up onto the heath, where the views are truly panoramic.

Ledmore and Migdale
© Andy Fairbairn

Glencoe Lochan

Glencoe
(NN104594) 137 ha (338 acres)
Forestry Commission Scotland

Created in the 19th century Glencoe Lochan, and the charming mixed woodland that surrounds it, was designed to replicate British Columbia by Lord Strathcona for his homesick Native American wife.

This beautiful setting is perfect for visitors looking for easy walking conditions, tranquillity and good views of the surrounding mountains. Visitors can choose the short circular all-abilities walk around the lochan or take one of two more adventurous routes through the forest of Scots pine, oak, beech and rowan, which include some breathtaking views over Loch Leven and the surrounding mountains.

There's an opportunity to fish in the lochan or enjoy a trip on an all-abilities boat. The National Trust for Scotland's Glencoe Visitor Centre (NN113576) is just 3.2 km (2 miles) away and has some pleasant walks nearby too. However, the paths and walking conditions can be hazardous in winter, when extra care is essential.

Glencoe Lochan
© Mike Carter

Rothiemurchus
Aviemore
(NH898085) 3,700 ha (9,143 acres) SSSI, NNR, NP
Privately owned
www.rothiemurchus.net

With spectacular forest and mountain scenery, exceptional wildlife, rugged, wild, and occasional treacherous terrain that's barely changed since the Ice Age, there's little wonder that Rothiemurchus has been extolled for its international heritage importance.

A vast array of natural habitats lie within the estate and its uses are just as varied; farming, forestry, wildlife conservation and recreation all meet in a way that protects the special character of the area.

The foothills of the Cairngorms contain some of Britain's least disturbed open areas of native forest. Its high plateaux, heaths and bogs, corries, screes and great boulder fields give way to deep glaciated valleys, burns, wetlands, high-altitude lochs and year-round snowbeds.

The Rothiemurchus Scots pinewoods are some of the most important, both for their wildlife and timber production. The regenerating Scots pines are nurtured and protected through an ongoing conservation programme, providing home for numerous birds including ospreys, crossbills and falcons, stags and red squirrels.

Visitors to this vast, ever-changing landscape can explore areas of woodland, enjoy off-road driving, fish in the loch, take in safari or family farm tours, try clay pigeon shooting and a host of guided and self-guided walks.

Among the array of interesting features, secluded and picturesque Loch an Eilein is a castle ruin dating back 700 years and provides an idyllic location for the visitor centre and shop.

Rothiemurchus
© Alph McGregor

Sunart Oakwoods
Fort William
(NM748617) 726 ha (1,794 acres)
Forestry Commission Scotland
www.sunartoakwoods.org.uk

Dominated by oaks the historic ancient woodlands of Loch Sunart, along the Gulf-Stream-washed west coast of Scotland, provide spectacular views over Loch Sunart and Salen Bay. The site can be enjoyed by people of all ages with different levels of walks and cycle routes, an all-ability trail, some hillier walks and a stunning wildlife hide and Gaelic alphabet trail, plus exemplary information boards every step of the way.

Golden and sea-eagles are seen in the area and the loch is renowned for protecting an important otter population. The woods themselves support a number of rarer species, such as the pearl-bordered fritillary and redstart.

Since 1996, a huge amount of work has gone into restoring and managing the oak woods for local benefit. The area is also home to some interesting Iron Age settlements, as well as a number of 19th-century clearance townships, such as Aoineadh Mor (NM668518) in nearby Morvern, cleared of its Gaelic-speaking people in 1825 to make way for sheep farming.

Nearby is the RSPB's Glenborrodale Reserve (NM600615), Salen Oak Woods (NM692640), Ariundle National Nature Reserve (NM828633) and Glenhurich Forest (NM814619) — all worth a visit while in the area.

Doire Donne
Fort William
NN050703 167 ha (412 acres)
SSSI
Scottish Wildlife Trust

Rarely visited by man, Doire Donne (brown wood) is an ancient coastal oakwood which rises from the north-west shore of Loch Linhe to open moorland.

Part of the Coneglen Estate, the site is dominated by sessile oak and birch, with ash, alder, wych elm and Scots pine. The thickest woodland lies on a steep raised beach and its deep shaded floor is covered in bracken, mosses and ferns. It's noted for its variety of butterflies and invertebrates which inhabit the thick, mature shrub layer and the mix of hazel, holly, rowan and

guilder-rose trees.

The chequered skipper butterfly and deadwood beetle are particularly rare residents. Others include roe deer, red deer, red squirrels, foxes, wildcats and pine martens.

Rumster
Wick
(ND215385) 1,000 ha (2,471 acres) SSSI
Forestry Commission Scotland

Set in a remote, hilly area, with views across to the coast, Rumster is buzzing with wildlife, especially deer and buzzards.

This pleasant conifer woodland has a mix of spruce, pine and sycamore, including a particularly huge sycamore which forms a feature of the picnic site.

Exploration is via a tar-surfaced pathway, which is generally easy going and offers the chance to spot ruined crofts and the remains of a broch.

Kintail & Morvich
Kyle of Lochalsh
(NG962211) 7,431 ha (18,360 acres)
National Trust for Scotland

Hailed as a 'walker's paradise' Kintail & Morvich, a conifer plantation of spruce and Scots pine, lies in a deep glen in the heart of a spectacular mountain landscape.

Die-hard walkers will enjoy exploring the more strenuous, higher levels, but for less serious ones, the going is much easier on the lower levels, where visitors can pause to enjoy the Kyle Straits and Falls of Glomach within.

Nearby is the coastal estate of Balmacara (NG796274) which offers views across to Skye and features the Lochalsh Woodland Garden, a favourite picnic spot. Although more garden than wood, the latter does offer lots of pleasant woodland walks and some 100-year-old beech trees to enjoy.

Lael Forest Garden
Ullapool, Laggan and Garve
(NH196806) 6 ha (14 acres)
Forestry Commission Scotland

Said to be a 'pleasant oasis' on the sometimes bleak road to Ullapool, native trees are gradually beginning to regain their hold in this small arboretum, which contains a collection of conifer and broadleaf trees from all over the world.

Golden eagles can occasionally be spotted overhead as you take an easy stroll through the oak, rowan and birch trees that thrive in this isolated mountain woodland.

Munro-baggers (the name given to people who enjoy climbing peaks above a certain height in Scotland) will want to visit Ben Wyvis while in the area, while less-active people might just want to take in the Rogie Falls.

Ben Wyvis Wood (NH412673) managed by Forestry Commission Scotland, is something of a Jekyll and Hyde in terms of terrain.

Visitors can enjoy a pleasant woodland walk alongside a small burn at the foot of Ben Wyvis, where the going is easy. But as you tackle the rocky climb up through the wood, which is made up of conifers, downy birch and rowan, the going gets more strenuous – despite the steps – and the views more dramatic.

Borgie Forest
Thurso
(NC666587) 3,000 ha (7,413 acres) SSSI (River Borge)
Scottish Ministers and the North Sutherland Community Forest Trust

Beauty, function and recreation all blend together beautifully in shape of Borgie Forest, an extensive area of mature forest.

Although a working forest, there's a strong community feel to the site, where the public is always welcome to walk, cycle, bird-watch or simply enjoy the beautiful location.

One of Britain's most northerly forests, it's still easy to access, and full of character with a dense cover of Sitka spruce, Scots pine and lodge pole pine.

Reelig Glen Wood
Inverness

(NH559432) 54 ha (133 acres)

**Forestry Commission Scotland
and the Kirkhill and Bunchrew
Community Trust**

Do you have a yen to see
Britain's tallest tree? Well, you'll
find it in the delightful

surroundings of Reelig Glen
Wood.

This dense, mixed conifer
and broadleaf site lies in a
narrow, steep-sided glen where
the going is easy, if occasionally
muddy, and the scenery takes
in a stone bridge and grotto
which lies at the head of the
trail. Visitors can take also take
a lovely walk along the
burnside.

Cawdor Forest
Cawdor

(NH848468) 159 ha (392 acres)
SSSI

Privately Owned
www.cawdorcastle.com

One of the Highland
Birchwoods, a great deal of
care and attention has been
lavished on the ancient

oakwoods of Cawdor Forest,
with recent restoration and
replanting work. Part of the
Cawdor Estate, it is owned by
The Dowager Countess
Cawdor and dates back
centuries. Rare lichens and
mosses are a feature of this
semi-wilderness woodland,
which can be explored via a
network of good trails.

Cawdor Forest

© Mike Carter

The Wildcat Trail
Newtonmore
(NN716984) 10 km (6.2 miles)
Newtonmore Community
Woodland & Development Trust

TV fans will recognise The
Wildcat Trail of Newtonmore
as the home of Glen Bogle, the
setting for *Monarch of the Glen*.

The site takes in various
habitats, from native woodland
to moorland and offers great
views of the Cairngorms.
The walking is enjoyable
without being arduous, though
it's hilly in parts. Trees to look
out for include larch, pine,
birch and alder.

Culag Community Woodland
Lochniver
(NC091217) 36 ha (89 acres)
Culag Community Woodland Trust
www.culagwoods.org.uk

A community-owned
woodland that offers magic and
beauty, Culag Wood provides a
wonderful coast-hugging
backdrop for the village of
Lochinver and the breathtaking
surrounding scenery.

Native species including
downy birch, hazel, rowan and
oak are complemented by
planted larch, beech and
sycamore; and there are
numerous quiet spots from
which to enjoy the tranquillity
and richness of this mixed
community wood.

A new path through lichen-
covered birches down to the
shore is the latest addition to a
series of routes running through
the site.

Inverewe
Poolewe
(NG863819) 6 ha (15 acres)
National Trust for Scotland

Great for children, with lots of climbs, twists and turns to explore, this mixed plantation woodland is an interesting blend of mature Scots pine – one dating back 100 years – and native broadleaves.

Rare glimpses of the Scottish crossbill and pine marten, plus panoramic views of the Western Ross landscape, may await visitors who follow the 2.4 km (1.5 mile) Pinewood Trail. Other residents to look out for are goldcrests, treecreepers, common hawker dragonflies and large red damselflies.

Visitors to the area might like to also visit the Laid Community Woodland just 8 km (5 miles) north, Inverewe Garden, Gairloch Heritage Museum and the nearby Pictish graveyard.

Inverewe
© NTS

177

The Black Isle

Brahan Dell
Maryburgh
(NH514546) 5 ha (12.5 acres)
Privately owned
www.brahan.com

June is one of the best times to visit Brahan Dell, a tiny part of the 1,618 hectare (4,000 acre) Brahan Estate, because you can then take in its spectacular collection of rhododendrons and azaleas.

Dating back to 1798, this arboretum of mature cypress, set in a mixed farmland and woodland designed landscape, features well-marked paths, which have recently been upgraded to accommodate wheelchairs. Look out for the rare Japanese umbrella pine, a large circle of big beech trees on an archaeological site, a giant redwood, plus other rare specimens individually labelled.

Alongside 12 km (7.5 miles) of riverside paths and more than 15 km (9 miles) of woodland walks, the estate also includes the site of Brahan Castle, home to the traditional chiefs of the Clan Mackenzie, self-catering cottages, a Caravan Club, fishing, mountain bikes for hire and guided nature walks.

It is also famous for the Brahan Seer, an estate worker who was put to death after (accurately) predicting the fall of the House of Seaforth. There are two monoliths to his memory on the estate and a number of Seer stones, as well as one at Craig Wood (see below).

Brahan Dell
© Mike Carter

Craig Wood
Avoch
(NH681553) 19 ha (47 acres)
Privately owned
www.craig-wood.gb.com

Part of the Black Isle path network, Craig Wood is an ancient semi-natural woodland dating back 200 years, which lines an old railway bed to Fortrose and has lovely views over the Moray Firth to Culloden.

In fact, the wood provides the only safe route for walkers and horse-riders between Avoch and Fortose, though the path can be muddy at times and visitors are warned not to cross any fences, as the site has steep slopes with 50-metre (164-ft) drops.

Dominated by oak, beech and elm, with some wych hazel, willow and hornbeam, the whole woodland is covered by a Tree Preservation Order because it features a number of large tree specimens.

An unusual carved beech stands close to the pathway, together with one of the Brahan Seer stones (see Brahan Dell above) containing an ancient inscription and prophesy.

Visitors may also like to visit the ruins of Fortrose Cathedral in Cromarty, Groam Museum in Rosemarkie, go dolphin watching at nearby Chanonry Point, or by boat from Avoch to Cromarty while in the area.

Drummondreach Oakwood (NH581574) is also nearby with beautiful views across Cromarty Firth, and the RSPB's Fairy Glen Reserve (NH735578).

The latter is a charming little glen near Rosemarkie. A relaxing little wood in a delightful setting, it has a burn running through the middle and an old millpond. Most of the paths are easy going, although people using wheelchairs may need assistance.

Craig Wood
© Mike Carter

Skye

Uig Wood
Uig
(NG394639) 19 ha (41 acres)
Woodland Trust Scotland

Next to the picturesque village of Uig is a bay, which is a gateway to the rest of the Western Isles. It is famed for

Uig Wood

© Mike Carter

being the most beautiful bay on the Isle of Skye and it is here that the Rivers Rha and Conon run down a steep-sided glen into the sea. This glen is Uig Wood.

Lying mostly at sea level, this charming little wood, which incorporates Conon Wood and Rha Glen, is rare in an area not famed for its trees. But, it's even more special because, as well as being the largest remnant of broadleaved wood on the Misty Isle, it contains many unusual species confined to the western side of Britain.

Some of the trees are relative newcomers to Scotland, like the giant sycamores, but many native trees are also present, such as alder, birch, elder, hawthorn, oak, rowan and wych elm. Growing together, these trees provide an important home for insects, birds and other wildlife to thrive.

There's also a link to very ancient woodland in the form of the stunted, gnarled and twisted hazel trees. True descendents of Ice Age forests, they cling to the precipitous gorge of the Abhainn Ra, surviving just out of reach of grazing animals.

Over the years, the Rha River has cut a deep gorge through the basalt rock and it now plunges down the damp ash and wych elm woodland via a series of waterfalls.

The Trust has put in a path so that visitors can get to the base of these falls and another path leads alongside the river Conon. These paths are narrow and steep in places, and can be both muddy and boggy at times, so care should be taken.

While walking here, look out for the lush growth of mosses and lichens, which the damp climate encourages. You might even be fortunate enough to spot a buzzard or if you're really lucky a seal bobbing about in the bay.

Shetland Islands

Loch of Voe
Lewick
(HU415625) 6 ha (15 acres) –
across all four sites
Shetland Amenity Trust

There is evidence to suggest that the Shetland Islands were wooded between the last Ice Age and the beginnings of Neolithic settlements when people first began to clear land for agriculture. However, after 4,000 years of sheep grazing and trampling, the Shetlands have almost no native woodland – just a few trees and shrubs that remain in the wild.

To reverse this trend, the Millennium Forest for Scotland project earmarked four sites on which to create new community woods.

The first small group of broadleaf trees was planted at Loch of Voe in 1986, but these have since been extended by a mix of exotic and native trees.

The other community woodlands are: Burn of Brae (HU358684) where planting continues to provide an attractive wooded park; the Burn of Valayre (HU370695) a steep, picturesque ravine dotted with waterfalls planted exclusively with native trees; and Burn of Twa Roes (HU847360) the most remote of all four sites, which flanks a steep burn and where native tree planting compliments the dramatic landscape.

Loch of Voe
© James Mackenzie

Western Isles

© Steve Liddel

Lewis Castle Grounds

Lewis Castle Grounds
Stornaway, Isle of Lewis
(NB416330) 243 ha (600 acres)
SSSI

Stornaway Trust

Said to be a perfect destination whatever the weather, the walks of Lewis Castle grounds, part of the Millennium Forest for Scotland project, are full of interesting features and views.

The walk takes in woodland, river, open moorland and shoreline, and from various points en-route you'll be able to enjoy views across the town of Stornaway, the harbour and the surrounding area.

To improve access to the 150-year-old grounds, extensive improvement work has been carried out to the paths and trails within the castle grounds, plus new bridges and walkways created. Restoration work is also taking place, with invasive species such as rhododendron being cleared and replanted with native species, to increase the diversity of the flora and fauna.

Isle of Eigg

Isle of Eigg Woods
Fort William
(NM475862) 263 ha (650 acres)
SSSI, NSA
Isle of Eigg Heritage Trust
www.isleofeigg.org

Unusual large for a Hebridean woodland block, the Isle of Eigg Woods offer excellent views across farmland and moorland. They consist of a variety of habitats, which are home to rich mix of wildlife, from woodcock to warblers, dragonflies to butterflies. Springtime sees this peaceful, quiet site carpeted in vibrant woodland flowers. However, the track is rough so walking boots are essential.

© Felicity Martin

Binscarth Wood

Orkney

Binscarth Wood
Finstown (between Stromness & Kirkwall)
(HY350140) 3 ha (8 acres)
Privately owned
www.walkorkney.co.uk

Trees are rare on the windswept Isles of Orkney, so the unusually tall trees that feature in Binscarth Wood make it an invaluable wildlife habitat, as well as being a green and shady haven for local people – and an island must-see for visitors.

One of Orkney's biggest plantations, although planted more than 100 years ago, the wood contains wild cherry and holly, but is dominated by beech and sycamore.

It's a popular site with nesting birds, and is extensively used by migrating ones. In fact, it supports 15 per cent of the island's regular nesting birds, being much used by long-eared owls and rooks. As many as 1,000 rooks have been seen here and it contains the largest rookery in Orkney.

The site forms part of the Orkney Walks and there's a firm, stony path through the wood, which is muddy in its lowest part near the burn that flows through.

Also worth visiting on Orkney is Happy Valley (HY327105) a sheltered area with a variety of planted trees by a burn. It's popular with local people, especially in spring when it's full of bluebells. The estate of Trumland House (HY432277) on Rousay also contains a walled woodland garden. The entrance is a short walk above the pier where the ferry arrives from Tingwall and there is a small charge for entry.

Orkney is also famous for the most northerly native wood in Scotland. Berriedale, an original wildwood relic, is a fragment of the woodland cover which Orkney would have once had before all the trees were cleared. The site is now owned by the RSPB and visitors are not actively encouraged due to its fragile nature. However, few people would make it that far anyway – it is quite remote from the nearest road, although one glen walk takes you within site of it.

WOODLAND
TRUST

The Woodland Trust

Established in 1972, the Woodland Trust is the UK's leading
woodland conservation charity.

We care for over 1,000 woodland sites across the UK, covering
20,000 hectares (50,000 acres). Access to our woods is free.

We want to see:
• No further loss of ancient woodland
• Woodland biodiversity restored and improved
• Creation of new native woodland
• An increase in people's understanding and enjoyment of woodland

If you have enjoyed this book and would like to become a member
of the Woodland Trust, give a donation or leave a legacy to us
please:

Visit: www.woodlandtrust.org.uk
or Freephone: 0800 026 9650

The Woodland Trust Scotland
South Inch Business Centre, Shore Rd, Perth, PH2 8BW
Tel: 01738 635829 Fax: 01738 629391
Email:Scotland@woodlandtrust.org.uk

The Woodland Trust is a charity registered in England and Wales (No. 294344) and in
Scotland (No. SC038885). A non-profit making company limited by guarantee.
Registered in England No. 1982873. It has obtained the consent of the Registrar of
Companies to be exempt from the requirement to use the word 'Limited' in its name.

Registered office: Autumn Park, Grantham, Lincolnshire, NG31 6LL.

The Woodland Trust's logo is a registered trademark.

Other guides in the series

The South West
of England

The South East
of England

The North West
& The Lakes

The North East
& Yorkshire

East Anglia &
North Thames

The Peak District
& Central England

Chilterns to the
Welsh Borders

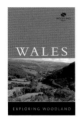

Wales

RRP £7.99

Prices are correct at the time of going to print and may be subject
to change. Please check current prices before purchasing.

TO PLACE AN ORDER PLEASE:

**Visit: www.woodlandtrustshop.com
or Freephone: 0800 056 0643**

Recommend a wood

You can play a part in completing this series. We are inviting readers to nominate a wood or woods, which they think should be included. We are interested in any woodland with public access in England, Scotland, Wales or Northern Ireland.

To recommend a wood please just photocopy this page and provide us with as much information about the wood as possible:

About the wood

Name of wood: _____

Nearest town: _____

Approximate size: _____ ha/acres

Owner/manager: _____

Their contact details: _____

A few words on why you think it should be included:

_____

_____

About you

Your name: _____

Your postal address: _____

_____

_____ Post code: _____

If you are a member of the Woodland Trust please provide your supporter number here.

Then please fax this form to us on: 01476 590808 or send it by post to: Exploring Woodland Guides, The Woodland Trust, Autumn Park, Dysart Road, Grantham, Lincolnshire, NG31 6LL. Alternatively, you can email details of your chosen wood to: woodlandguides@woodlandtrust.org.uk
Thank you for your help.

Getting there

You can find out how to get to the sites listed in this guide by putting the relevant grid reference into an online mapping program (such as www.multimap.com at a scale of 1:25,000). The grid reference will either give you the point at the centre of the wood or often, its main entrance or car park.

Alternatively, on the following pages you will find telephone numbers and website addresses for all the organisations that own or manage woods listed in this book. In most cases, these will give you additional information, locations and directions to the woodland sites listed herein. For privately-owned sites, website addresses, where available, are printed next to the relevant wood entry.

The Woodland Trust's online woods directory, also gives more detailed information on locations, access and facilities for all our sites. For more details visit: www.woodlandtrust.org.uk/woods

Your nearest library will usually provide free access to the Internet plus advice and training. Your local telephone directory will give details of your nearest library. Alternatively visit: www.direct.gov.uk

As an environmental organisation, the Woodland Trust tries to encourage visitors to travel, where possible, by public transport.

Traveline provides impartial journey planning information for public transport services. You can contact them by ringing 0871 200 2233 (calls charged at national rates) or by visiting their website at www.traveline.org.uk

For details about the Sustrans Cycle Network please telephone: 0845 113 0065 or visit: www.sustrans.org.uk

Further information

Borders Forest Trust, 01835 830 750, www.bordersforesttrust.org
Central Scotland Forest Trust, www.csft.org.uk
Community Woodland Association, 01854 613 737,
    www.community-woods.org.uk
Core Forests, 01463 811 606, www.coreforestsites.co.uk
The Crown Estate, 0131 260 6070, www.thecrownestate.co.uk
Forestry Commission Scotland, 0845 367 3787,
    www.forestry.gov.uk/scotland
Highland Birchwoods, 01463 811 606,
    www.highlandbirchwoods.co.uk
John Muir Trust, 0131 554 0114, www.jmt.org
Millennium Forest Trust for Scotland,
    enquiries@millenniumforest.org.uk,
    www.millenniumforest.co.uk
National Trust for Scotland, 0844 493 2100, www.nts.org.uk
Native Woodland Discussion Group, www.nwdg.org.uk
Perthshire Big Tree Country, www.perthshirebigtreecountry.co.uk
RSPB Scotland, 01767 680 551, www.rspb.org.uk/scotland
Scottish Natural Heritage, 01463 725 000, www.snh.org.uk
Scottish Wildlife Trust, 0131 312 7765, www.swt.org.uk
Scottish Forest Alliance, www.scottishforestalliance.org.uk
The Woodland Trust, 01476 581 111, www.woodlandtrust.org.uk
Visit Scotland, 0845 225 5121, www.visitscotland.com

Scottish Councils

Aberdeen City, 01224 522 000, www.aberdeencity.gov.uk
Aberdeenshire, 0845 081 207, www.aberdeenshire.gov.uk
Angus, 08452 777 778, www.angus.gov.uk
Argyll and Bute, 01546 602 127, www.argyll-bute.gov.uk
Clackmannanshire, 01259 450 000, www.clacksweb.org.uk
Dumfries and Galloway, 01387 260 000, www.dumgal.gov.uk
Dundee City, 01382 434 800, www.dundeecity.gov.uk
East Ayrshire, 0845 724 0000, www.east-ayrshire.gov.uk
East Dunbartonshire, 0845 045 4510, www.eastdunbarton.gov.uk
East Lothian, 01620 827 827, www.eastlothian.gov.uk
East Renfrewshire, 01415 773 001, www.eastrenfrewshire.gov.uk
Edinburgh City, 01312 002 323, www.edinburgh.gov.uk
Falkirk, 01324 506 070, www.falkirk.gov.uk
Fife, 08451 550 000, www.fifedirect.gov.uk
Glasgow City, 01412 872 000, www.glasgow.gov.uk
Highland, 01463 702 000, www.highland.gov.uk
Inverclyde, 01475 717 171, www.inverclyde.gov.uk
Midlothian, 01312 707 500, www.midlothian.gov.uk
Moray, 01343 543 451, www.moray.gov.uk
North Ayrshire, 0845 603 0590, www.north-ayrshire.gov.uk
North Lanarkshire, 01698 403 200, www.northlan.gov.uk
Orkney Islands, 01856 873 535, www.orkney.gov.uk
Perth and Kinross, 01738 475 000, www.pkc.gov.uk
Renfrewshire, 01418 425 000, www.renfrewshire.gov.uk
Scottish Borders, 01835 824 000, www.scotborders.gov.uk
Shetland Islands, 01595 693 535, www.shetland.gov.uk
South Ayrshire, 0845 601 2020, www.south-ayrshire.gov.uk
South Lanarkshire, 01698 454 444, www.southlanarkshire.gov.uk
Stirling, 0845 277 7000, www.stirling.gov.uk
West Dunbartonshire, 01389 737 000, www.wdcweb.info
West Lothian, 01506 775 000, www.wlonline.org
Western Isles, 01851 703 773, www.w-isles.gov.uk

Index